This Book Belongs To:

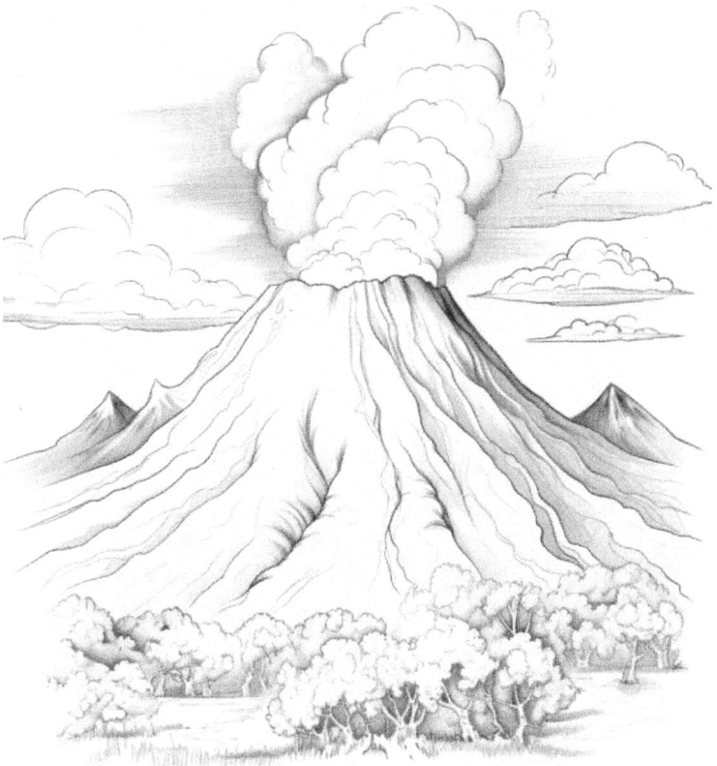

IMAGINE THAT!

studio

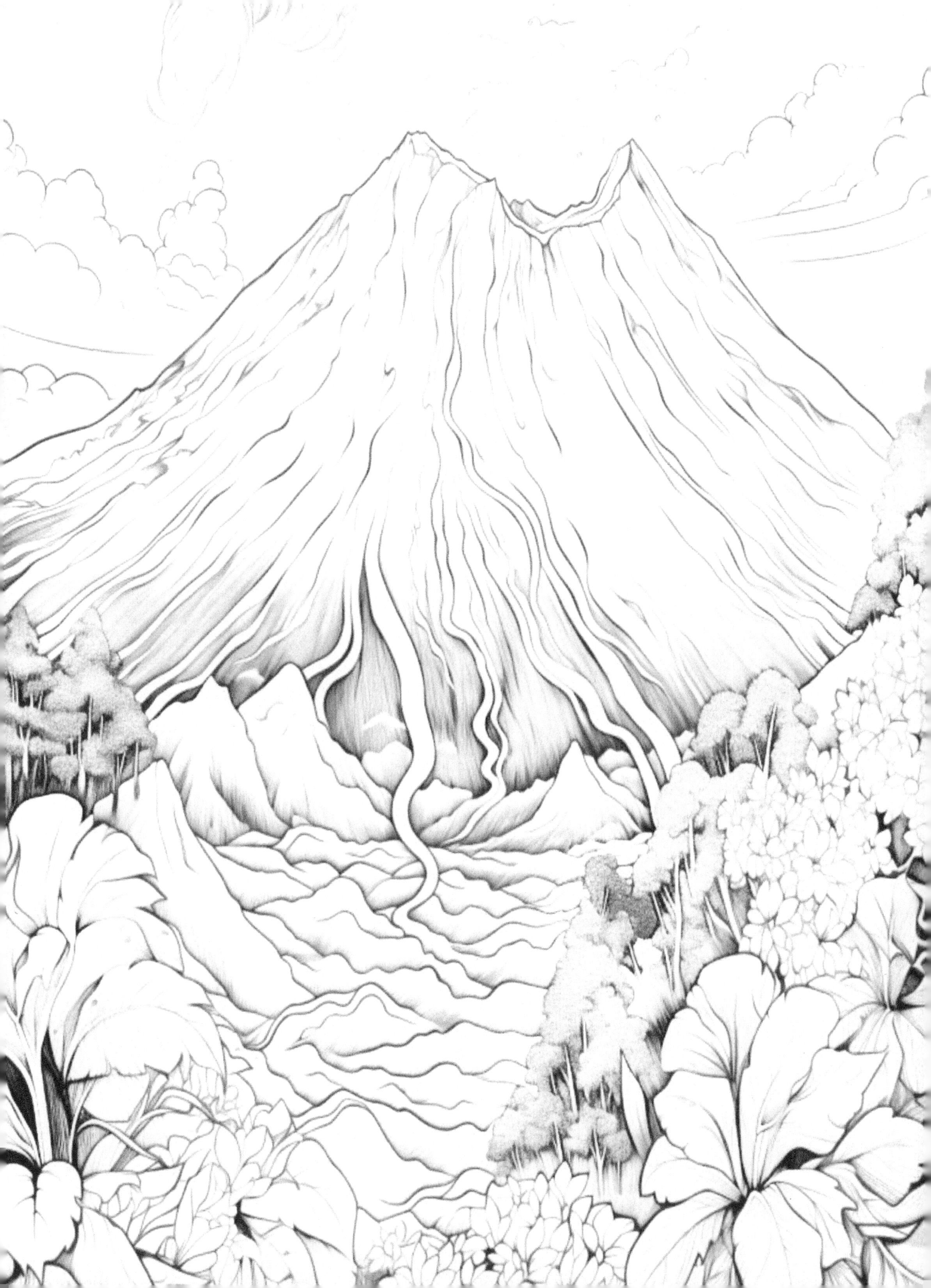

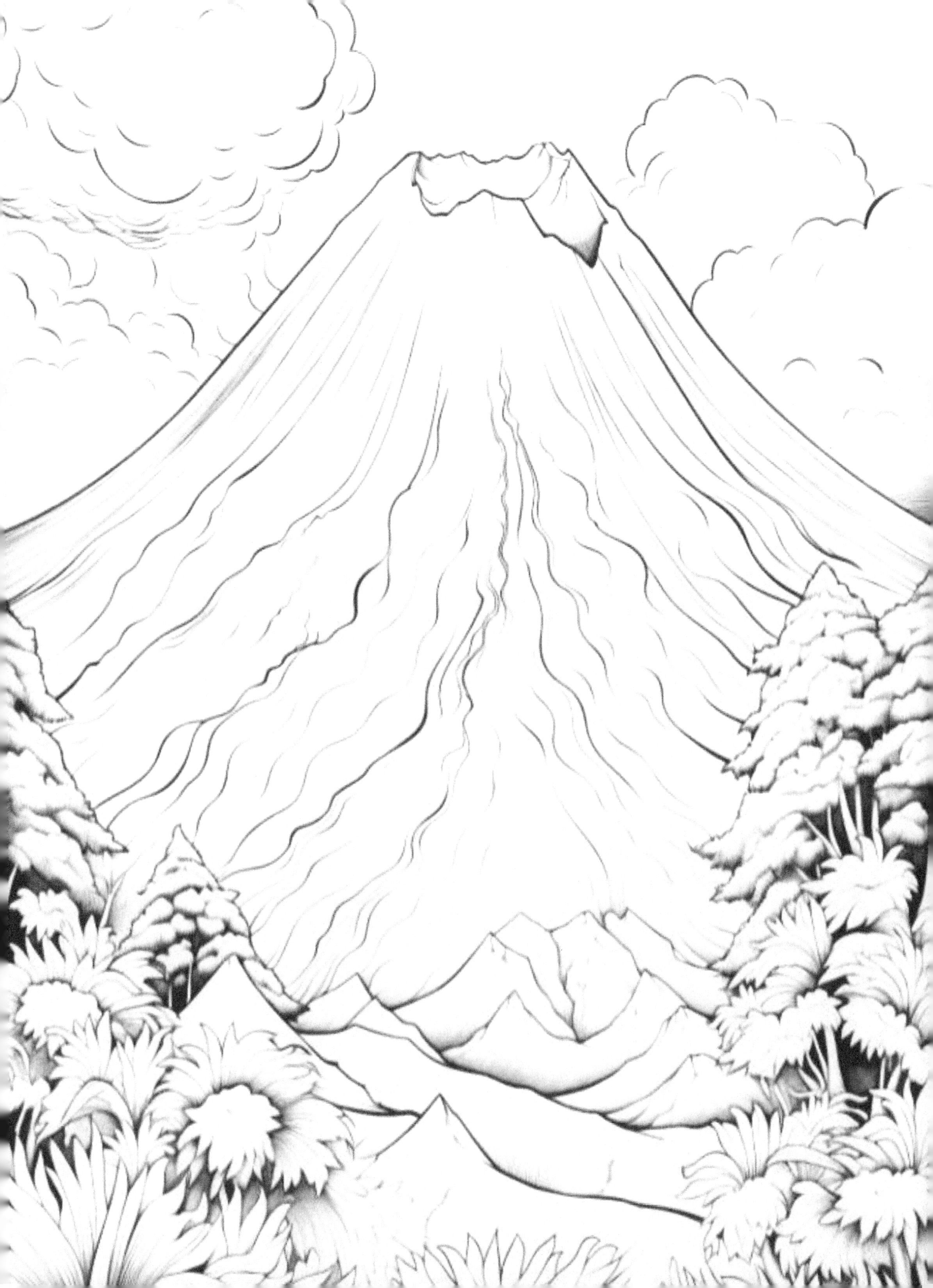

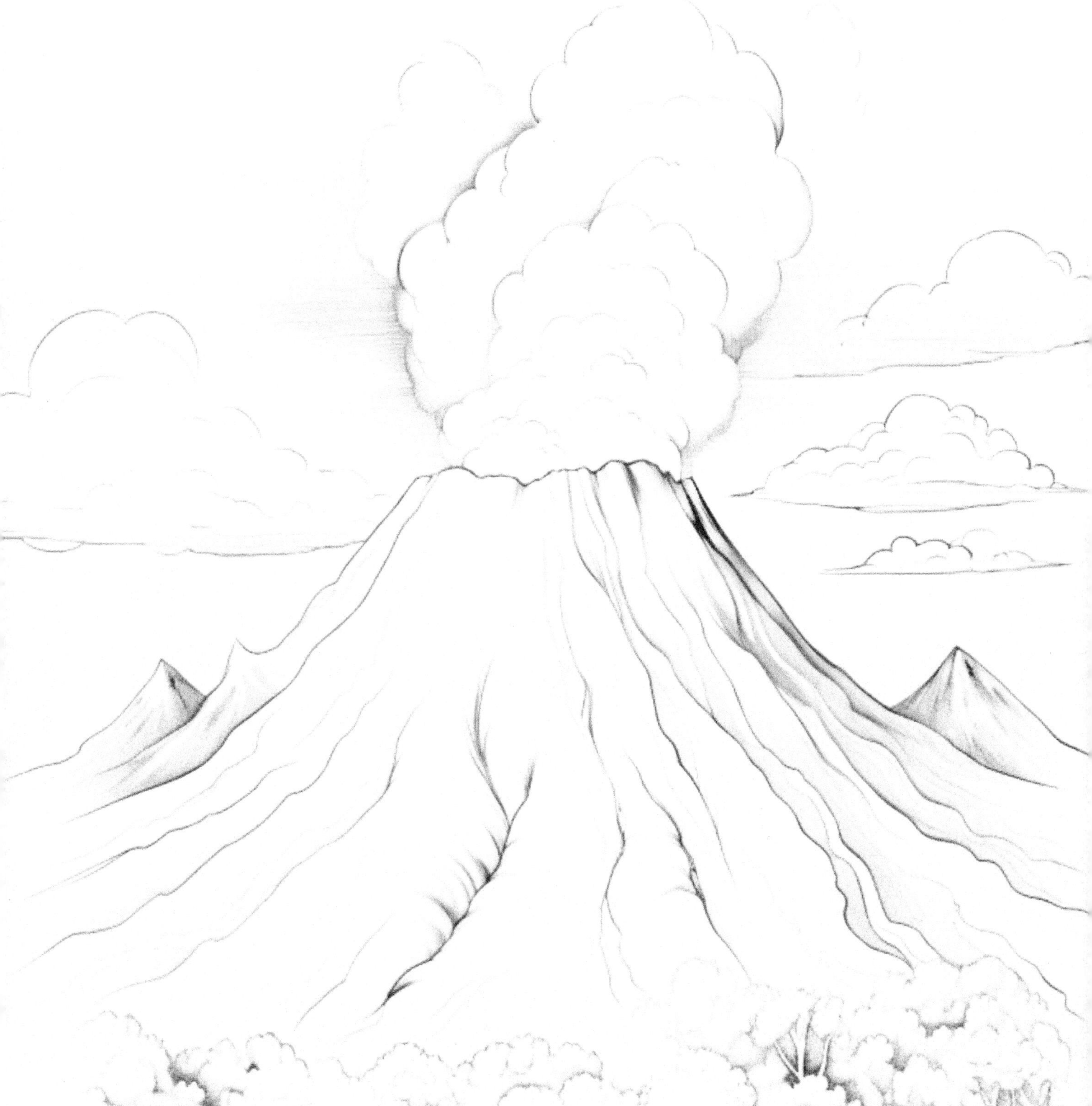

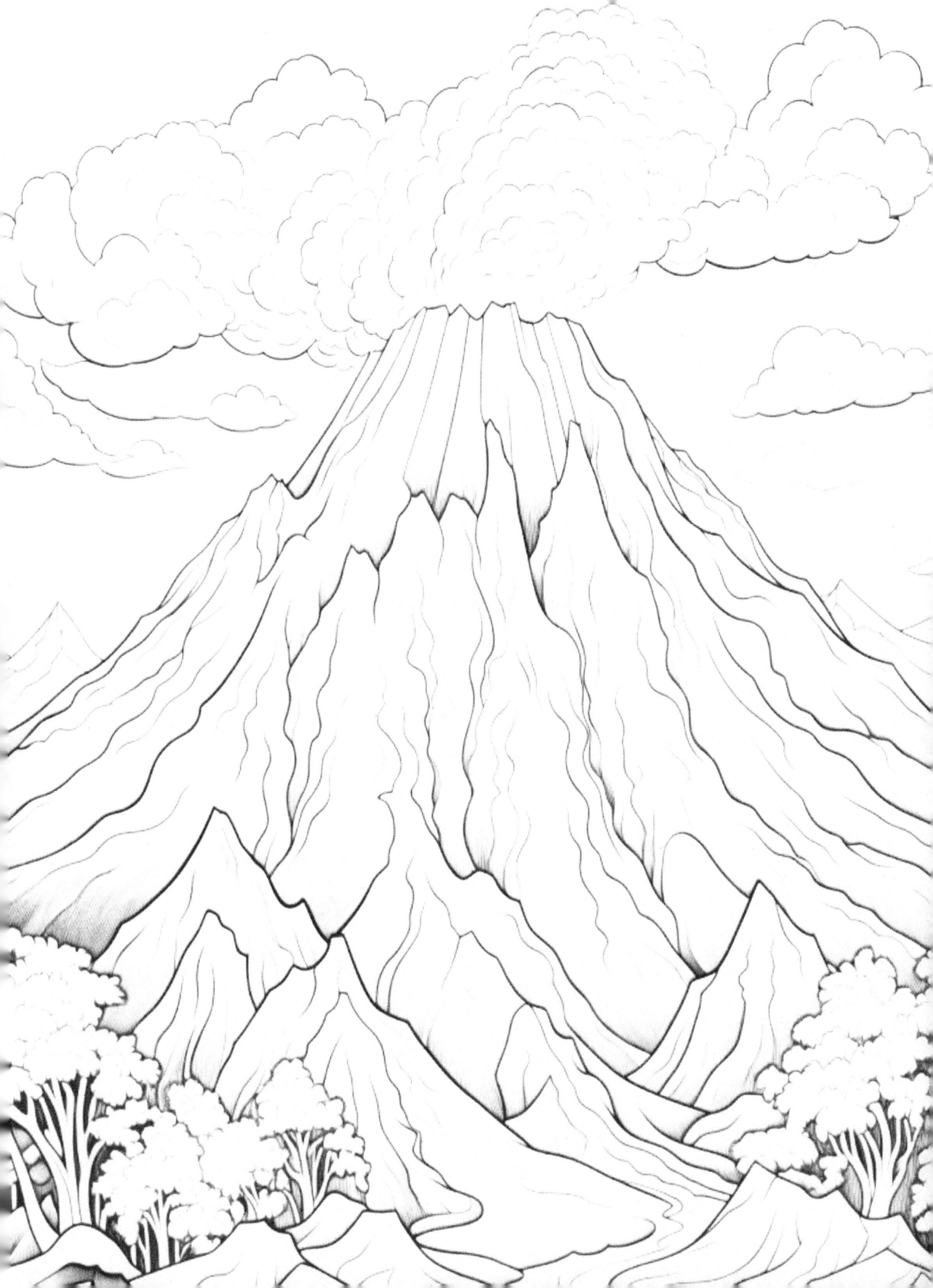

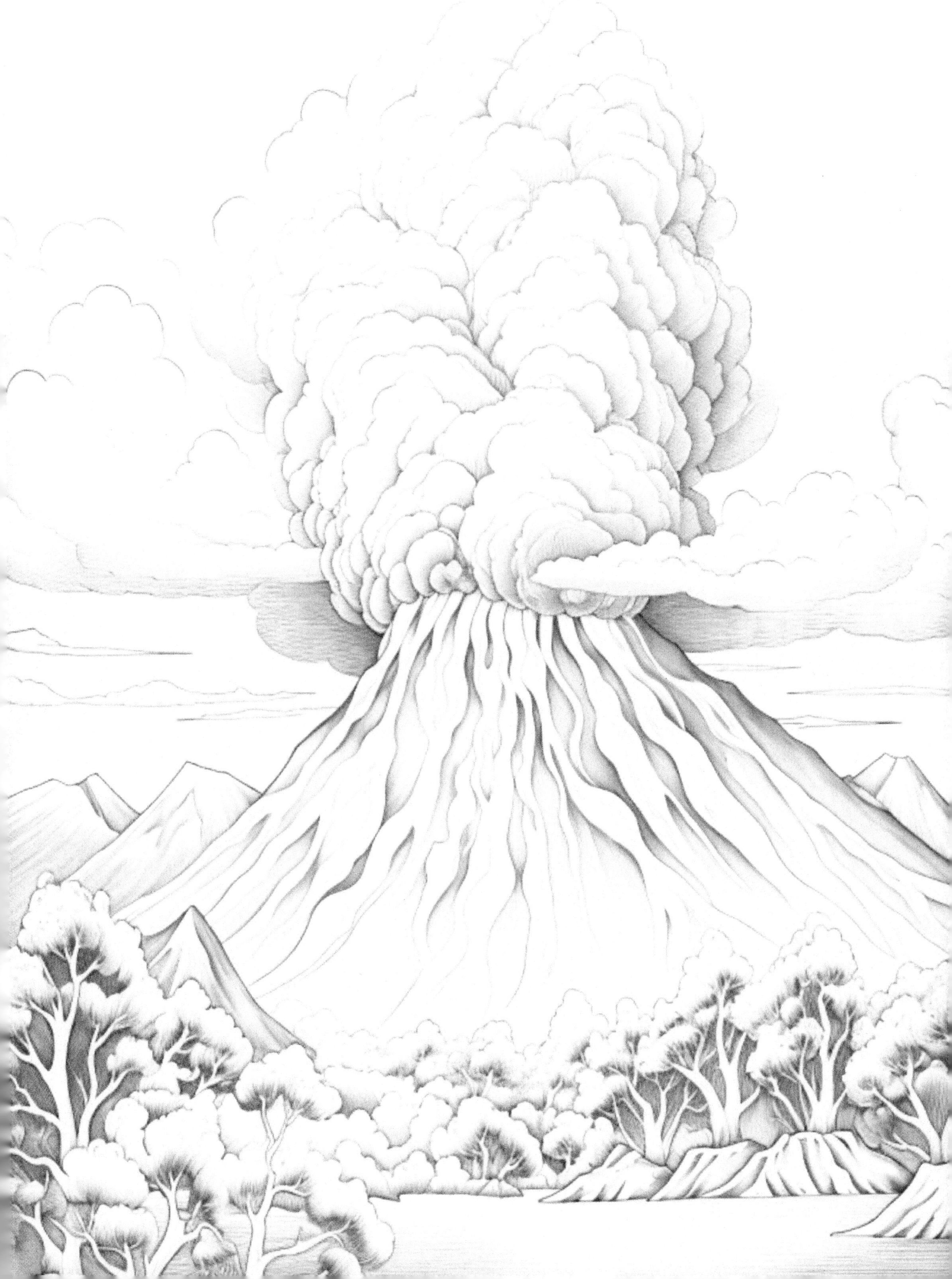

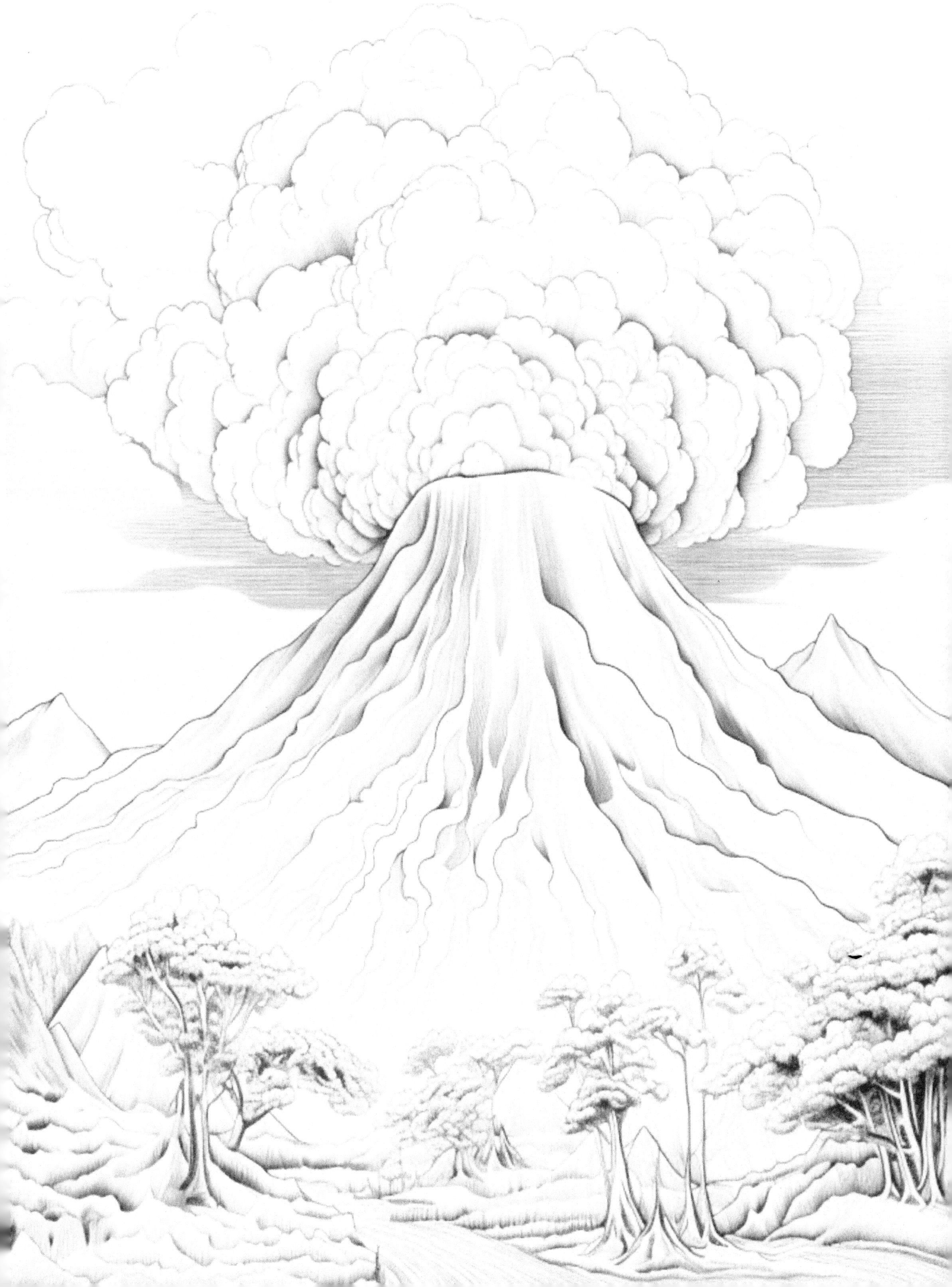

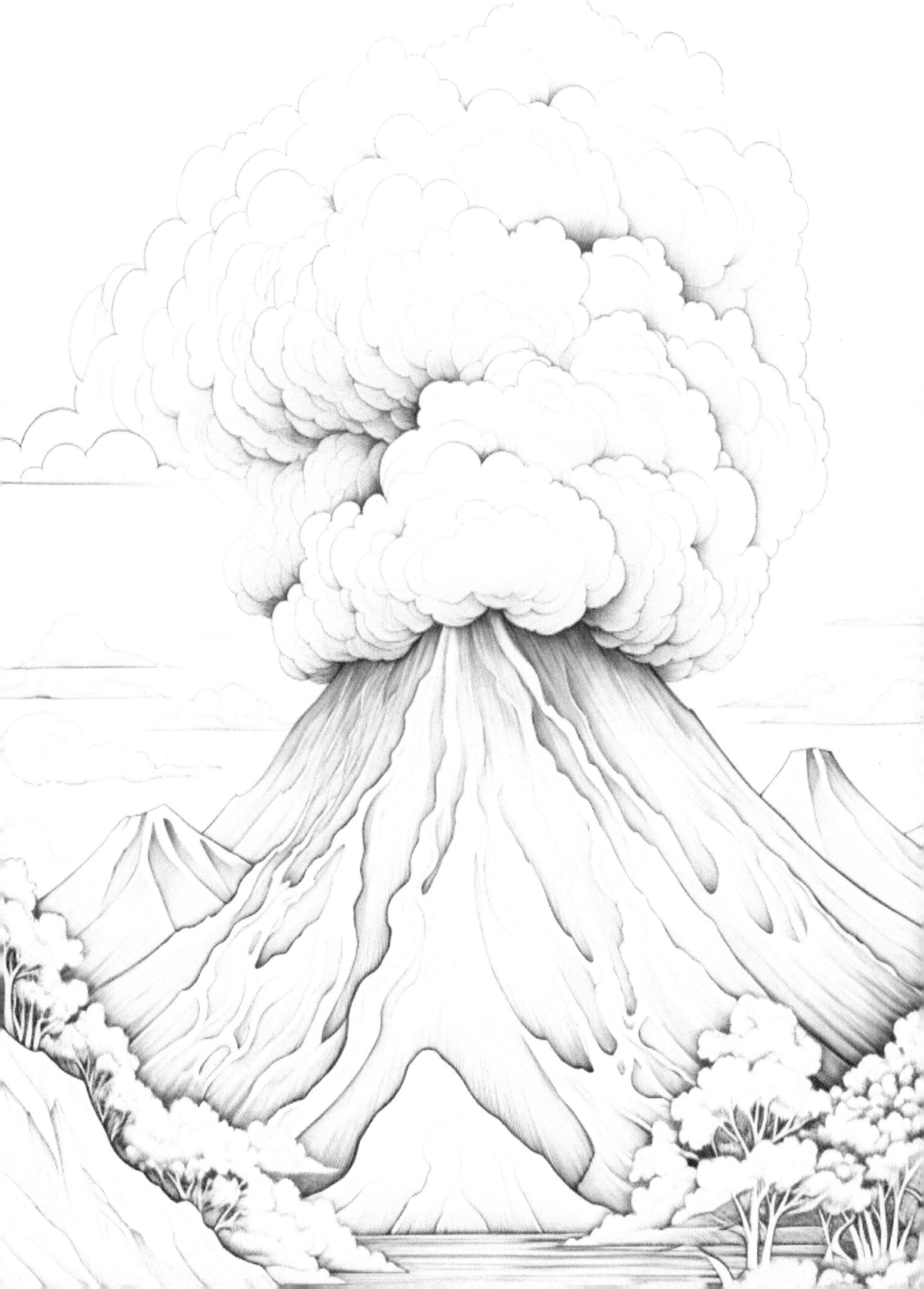

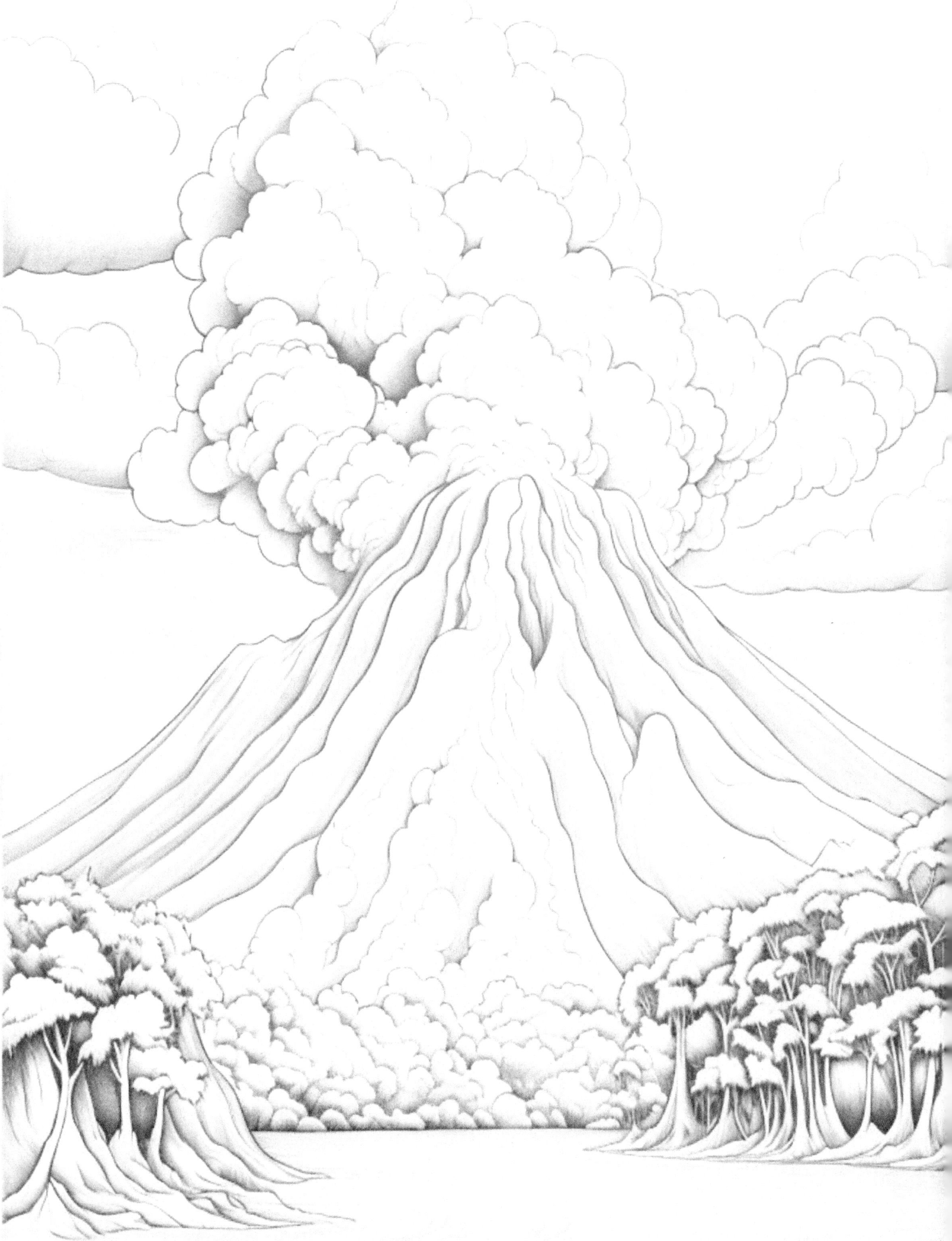

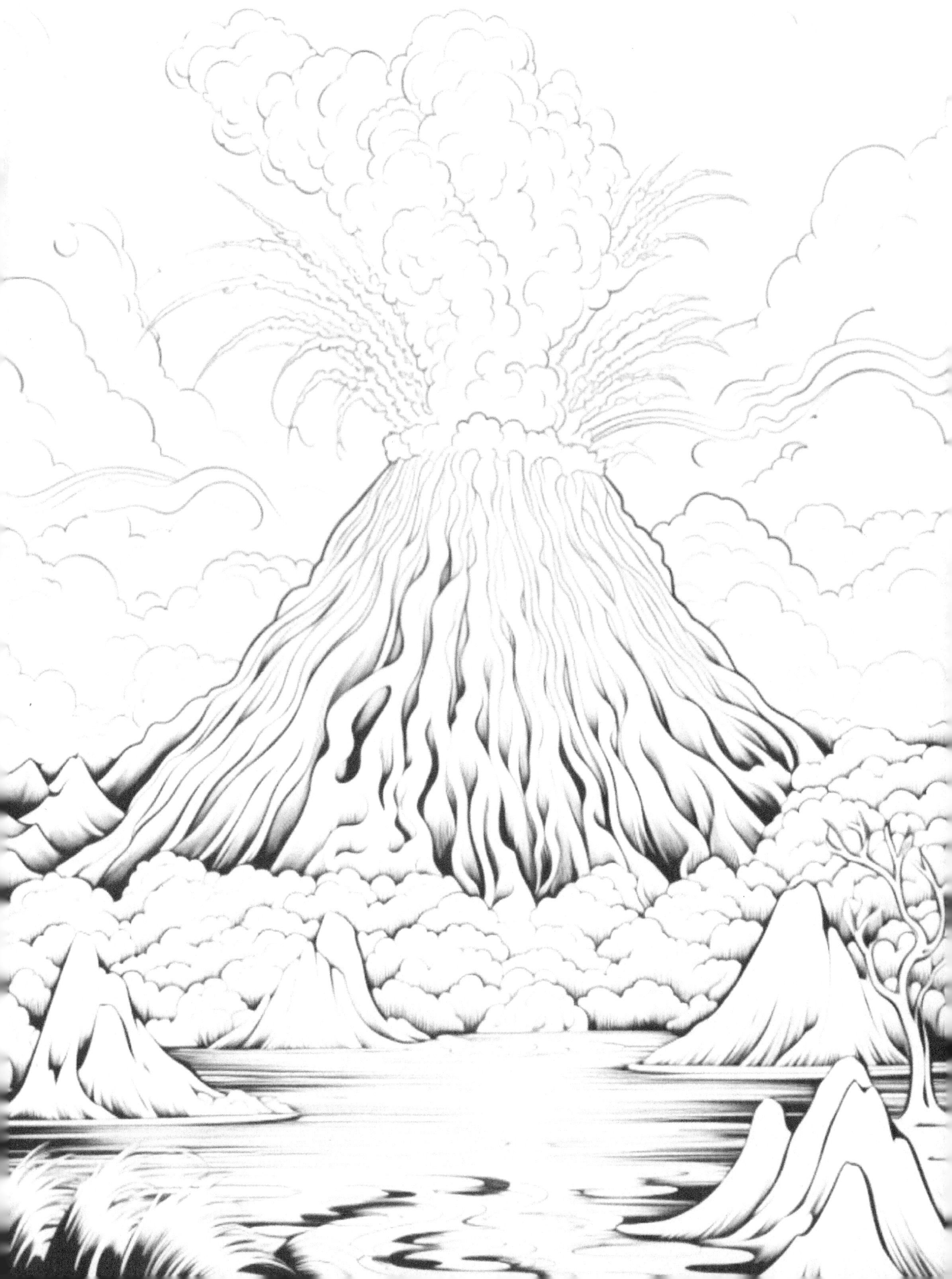

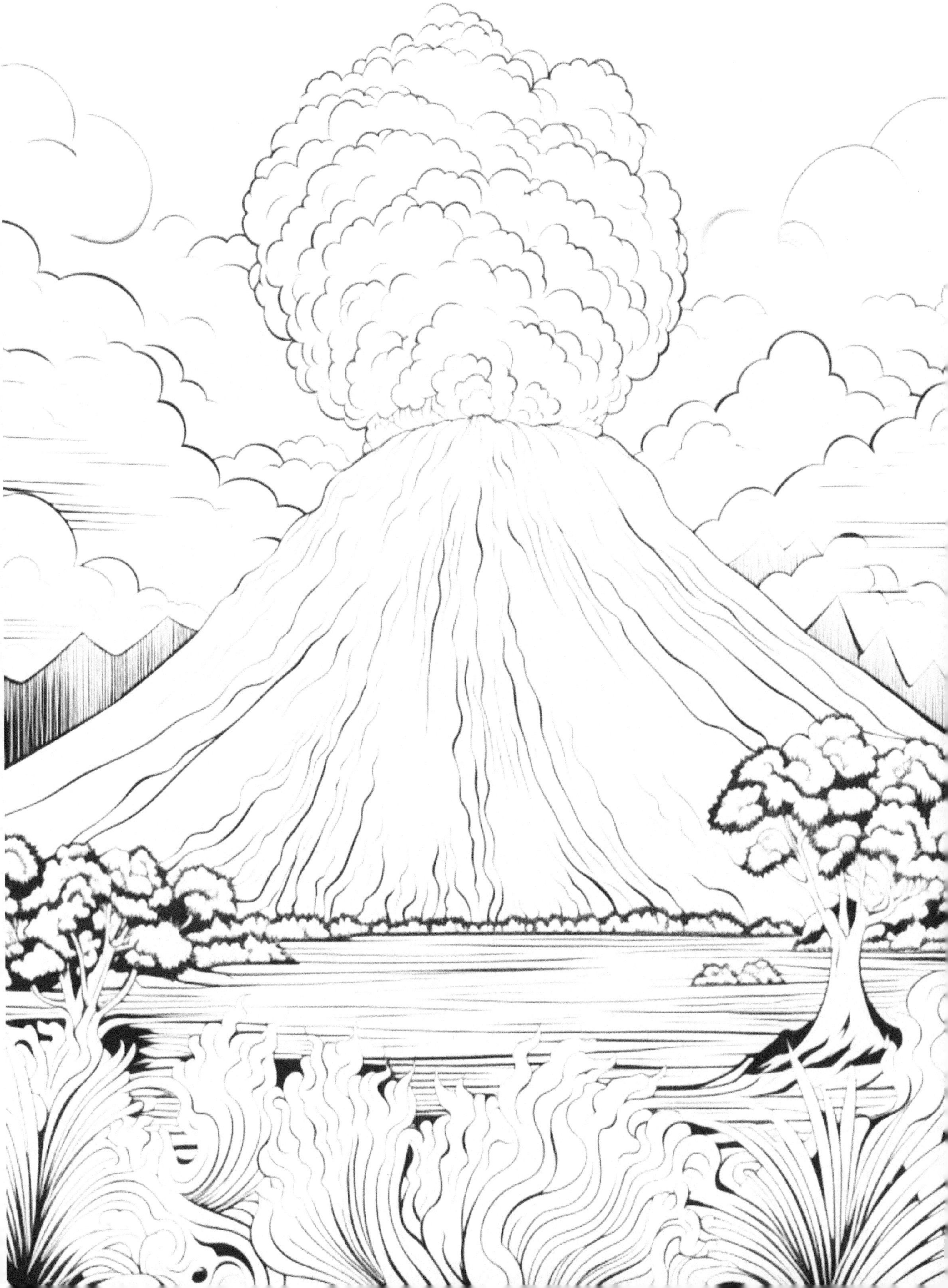

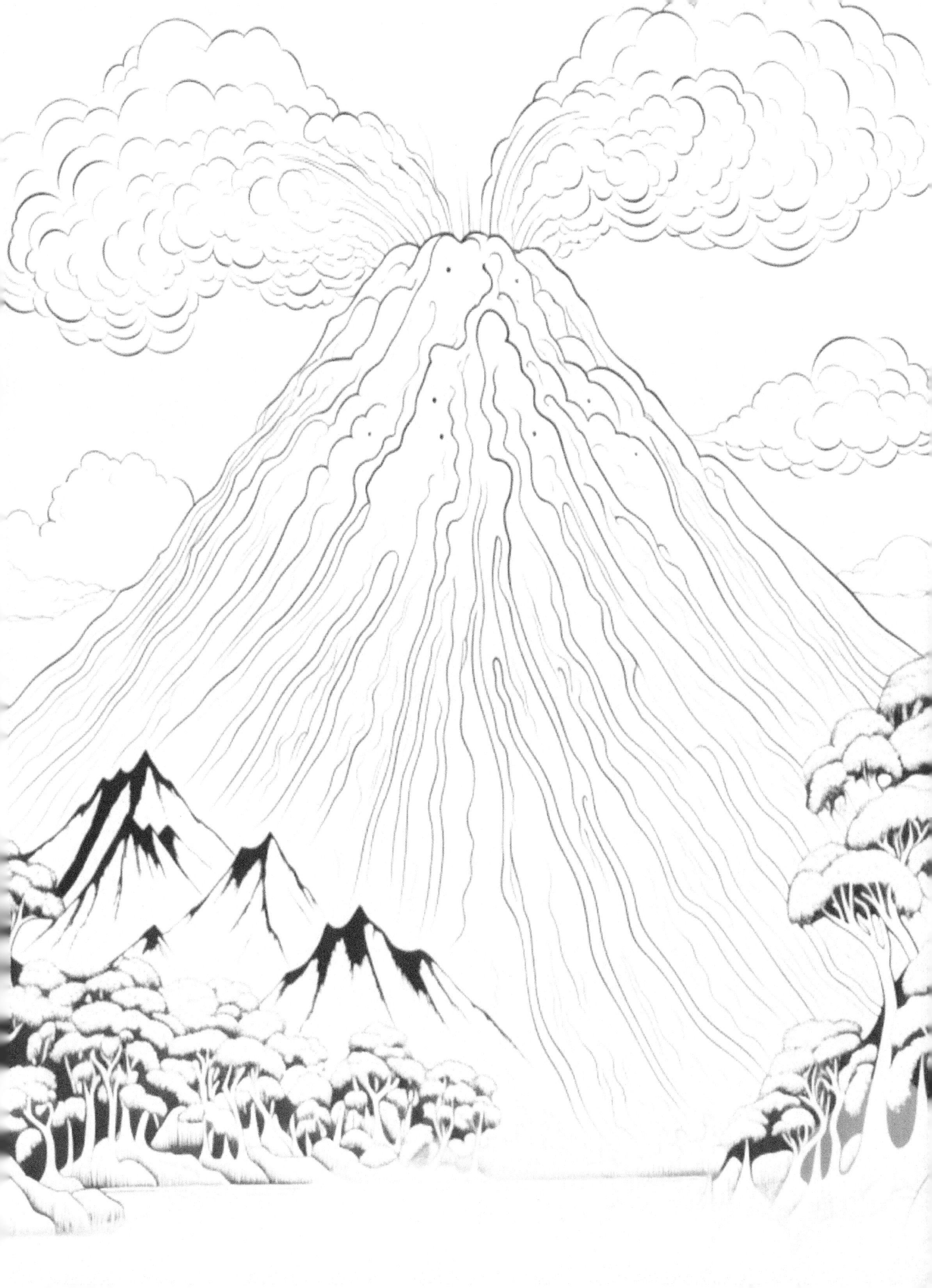

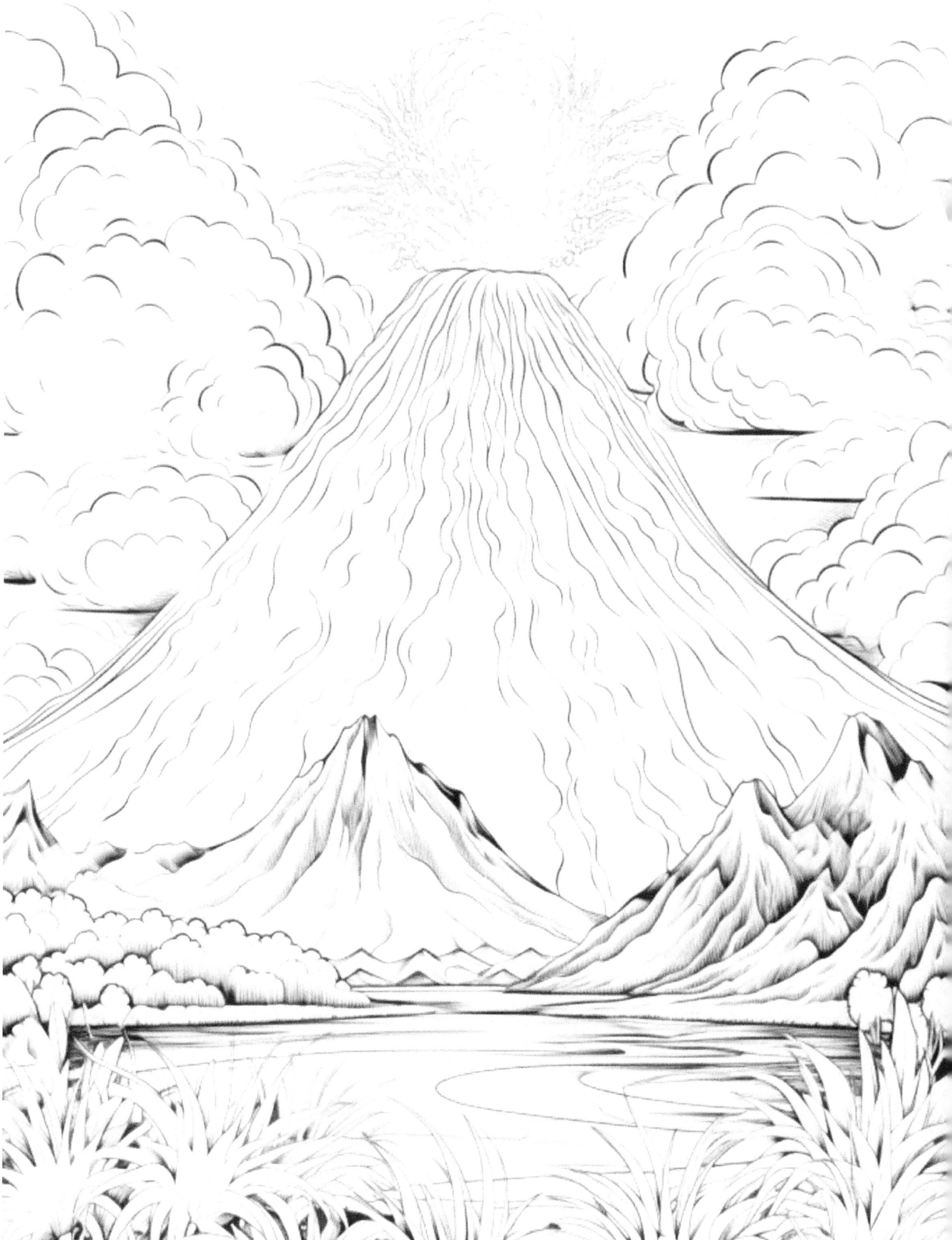

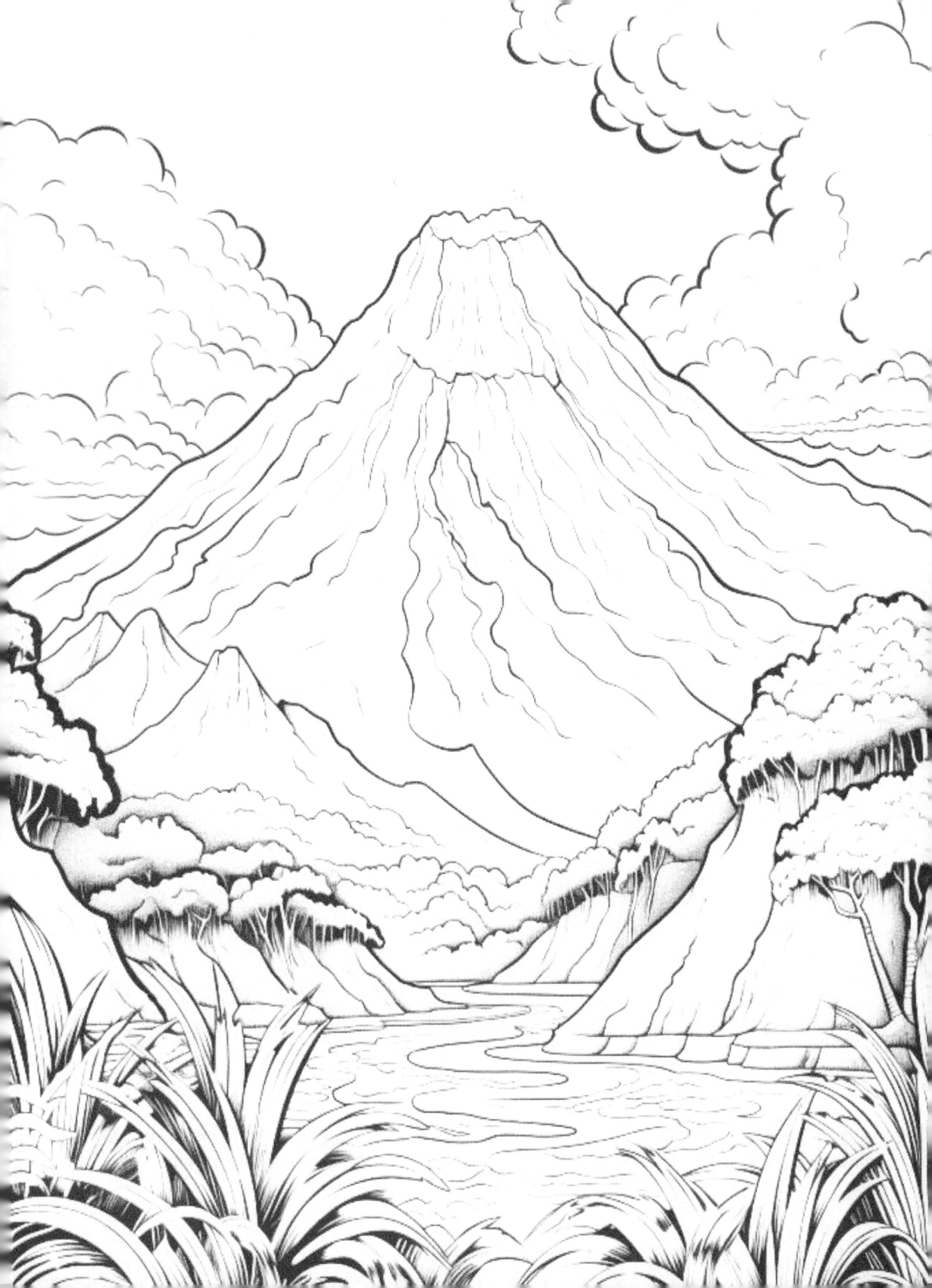

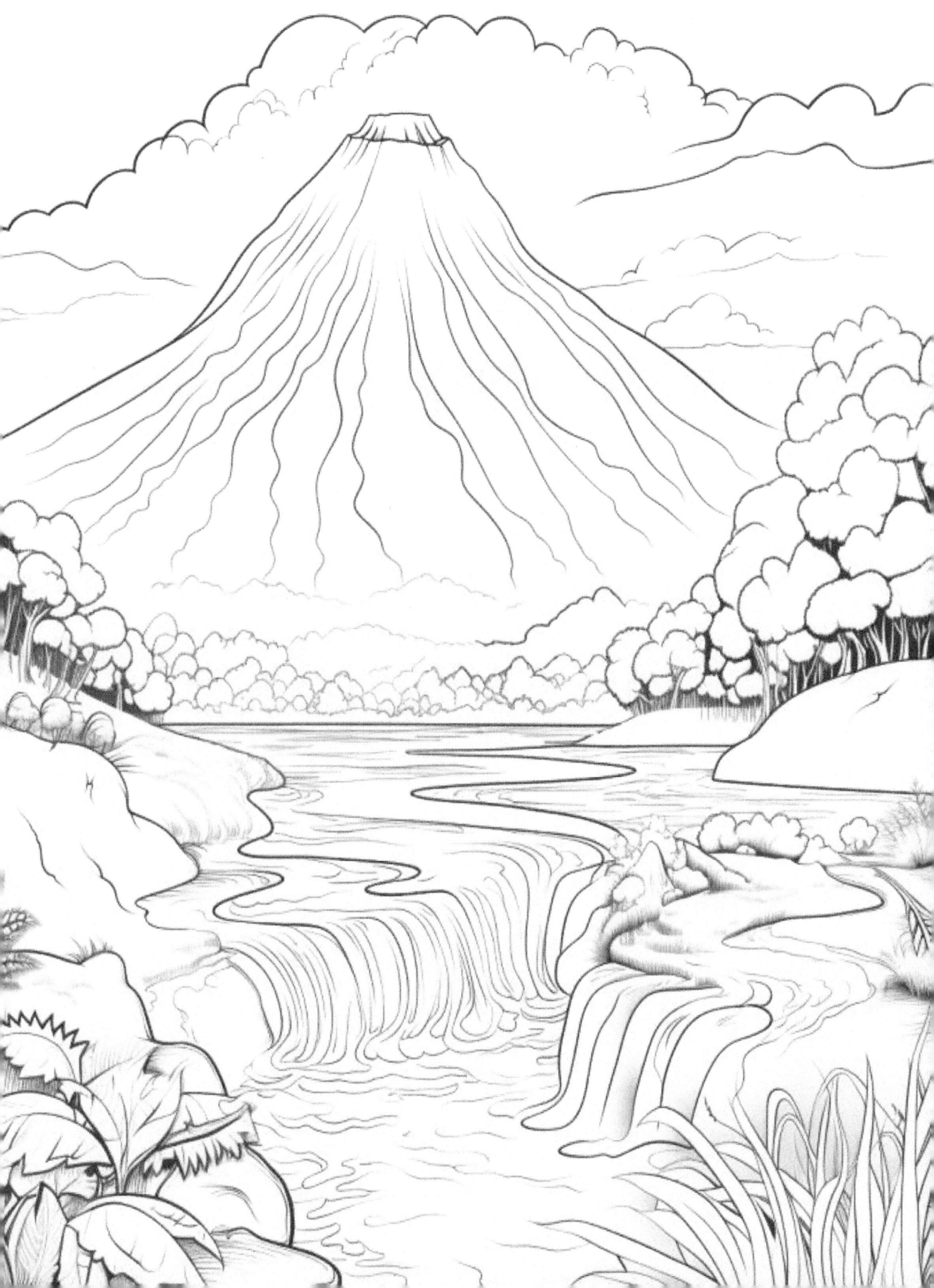

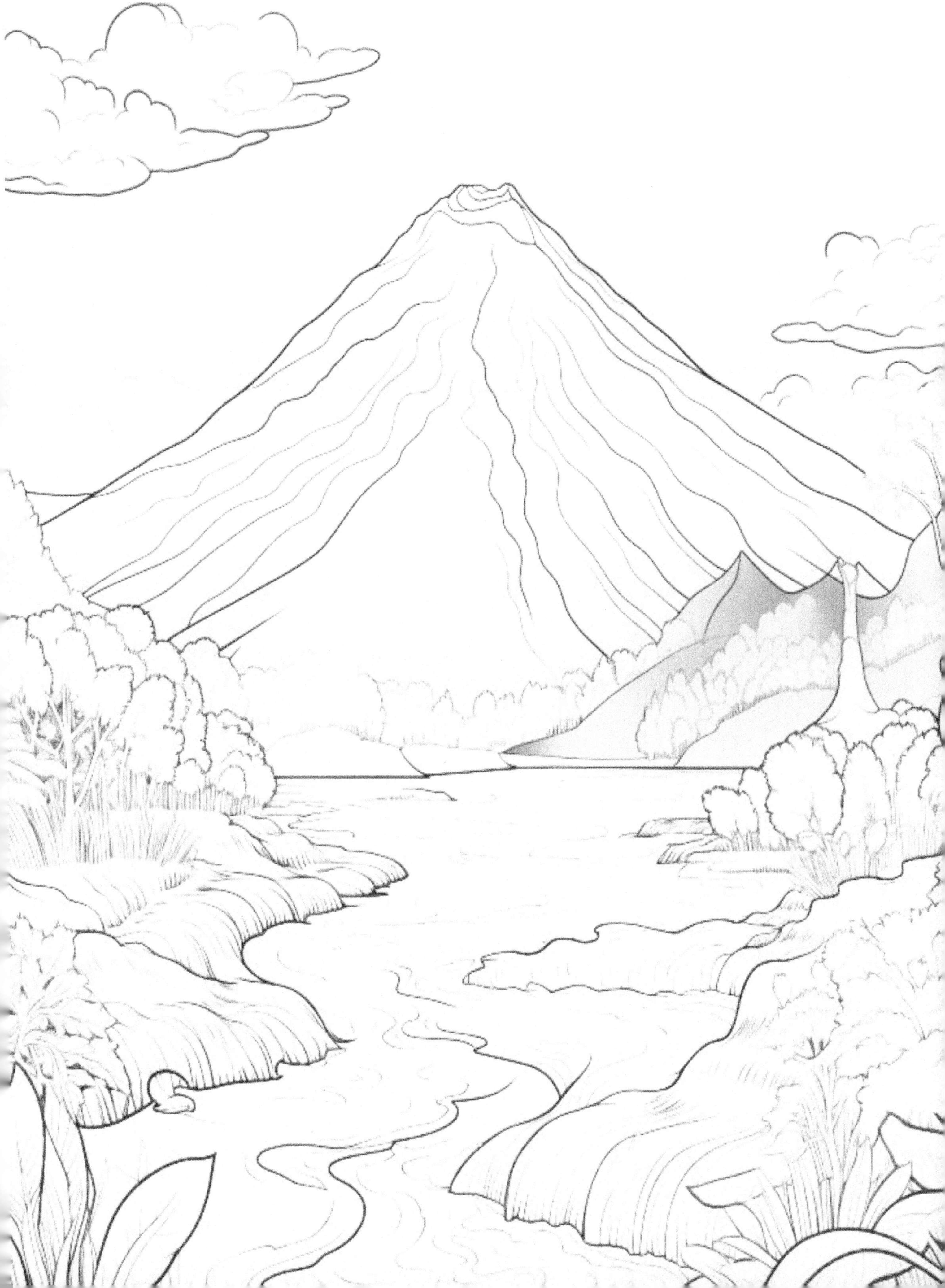

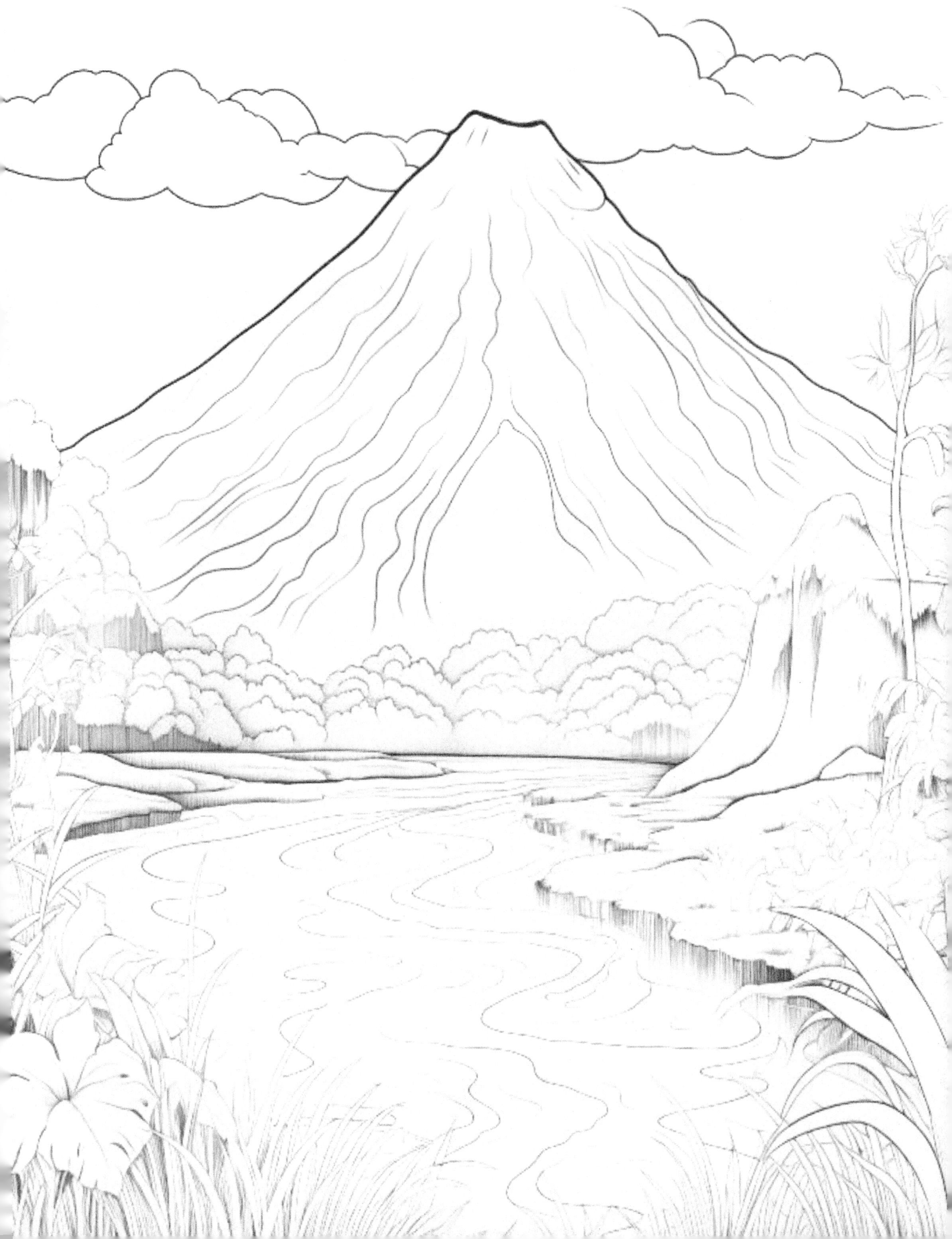

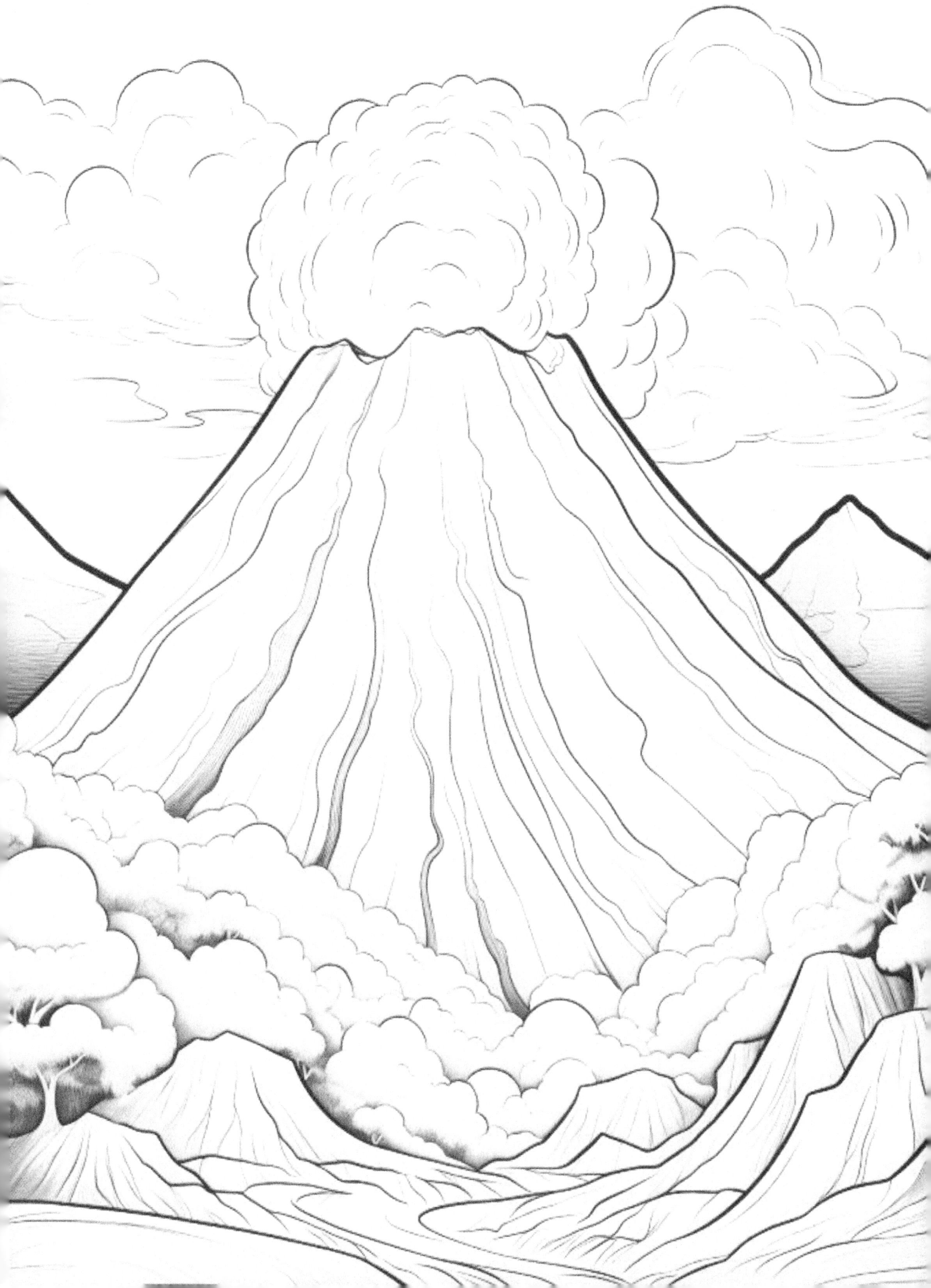

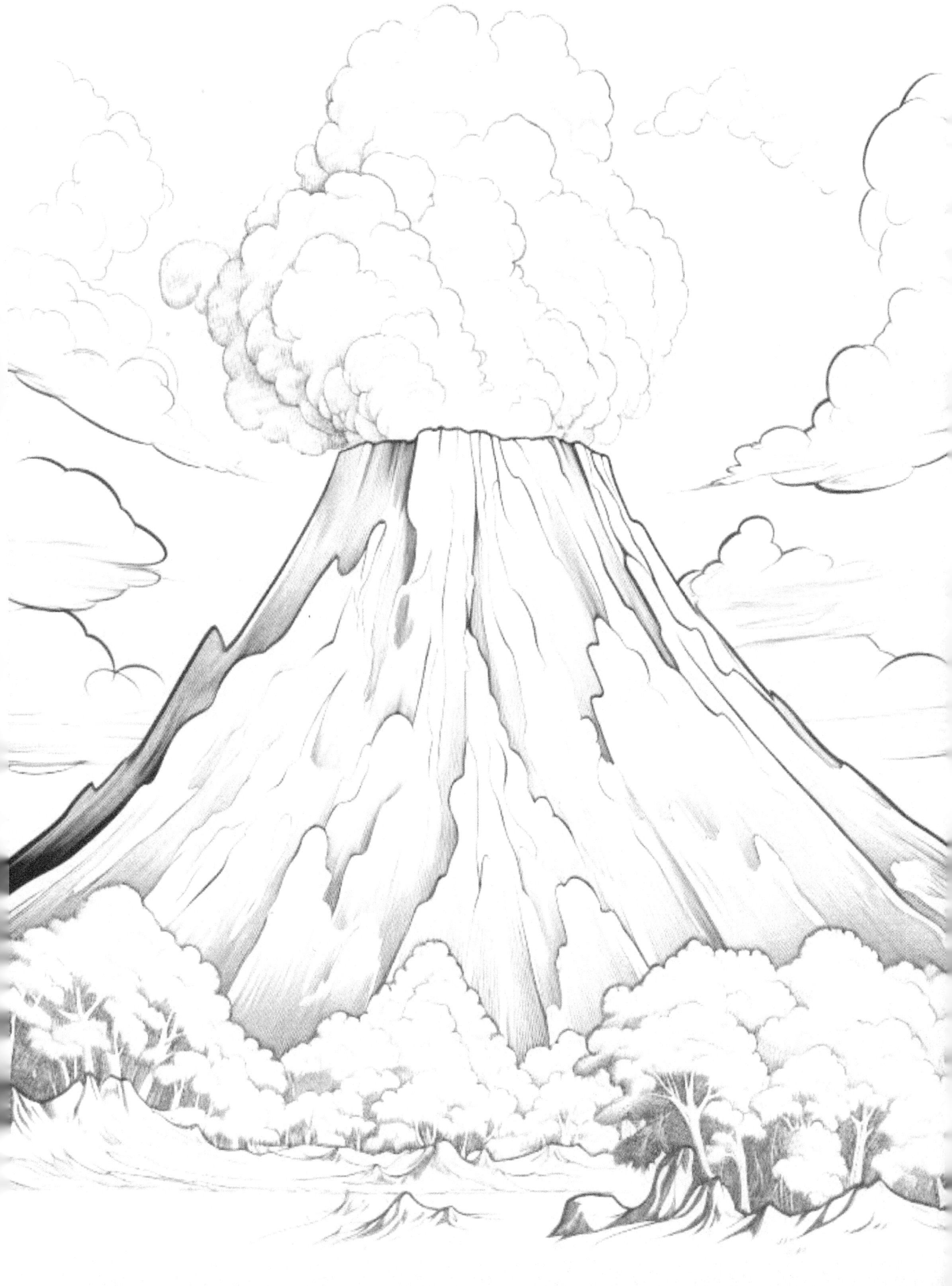

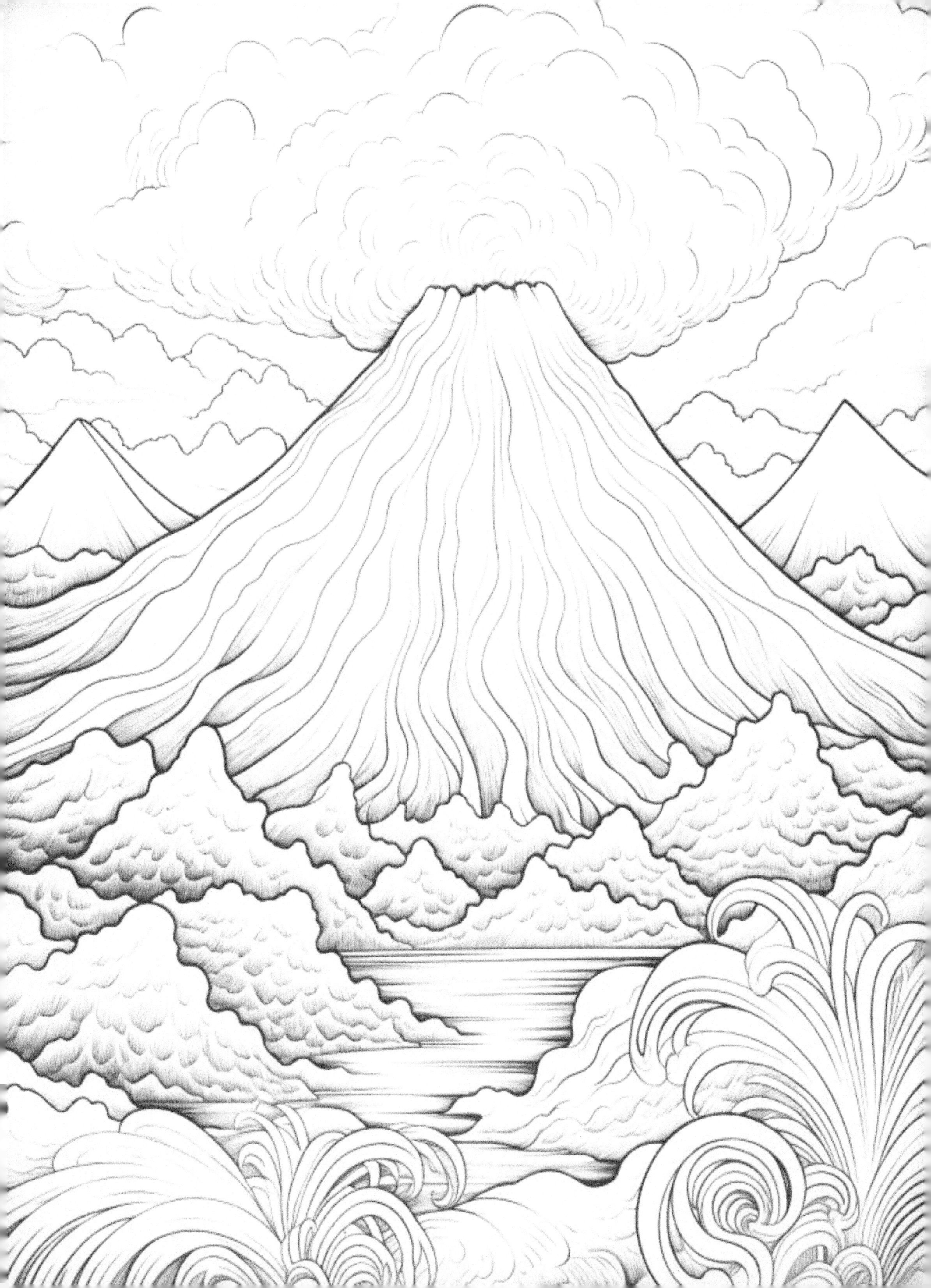

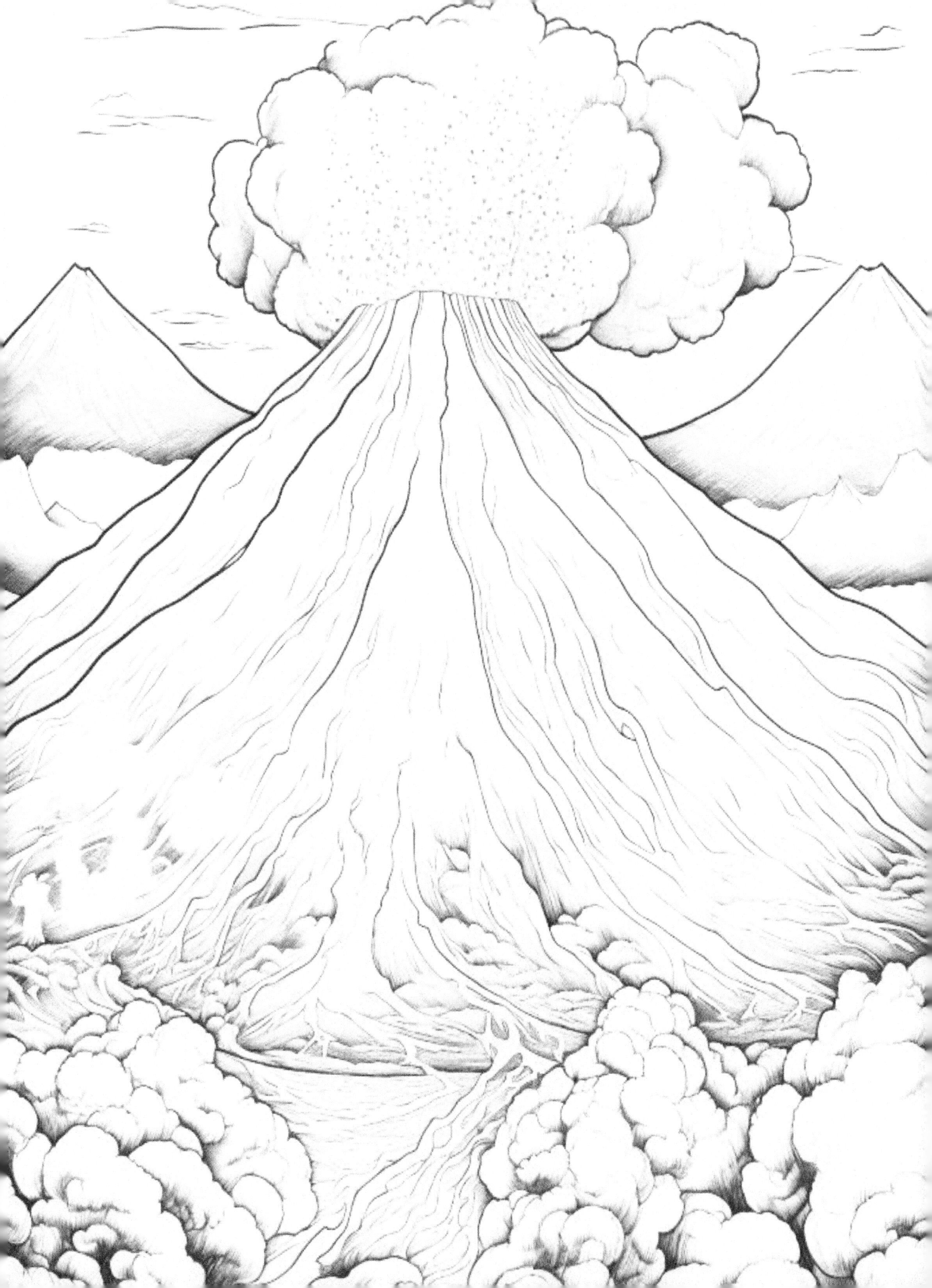

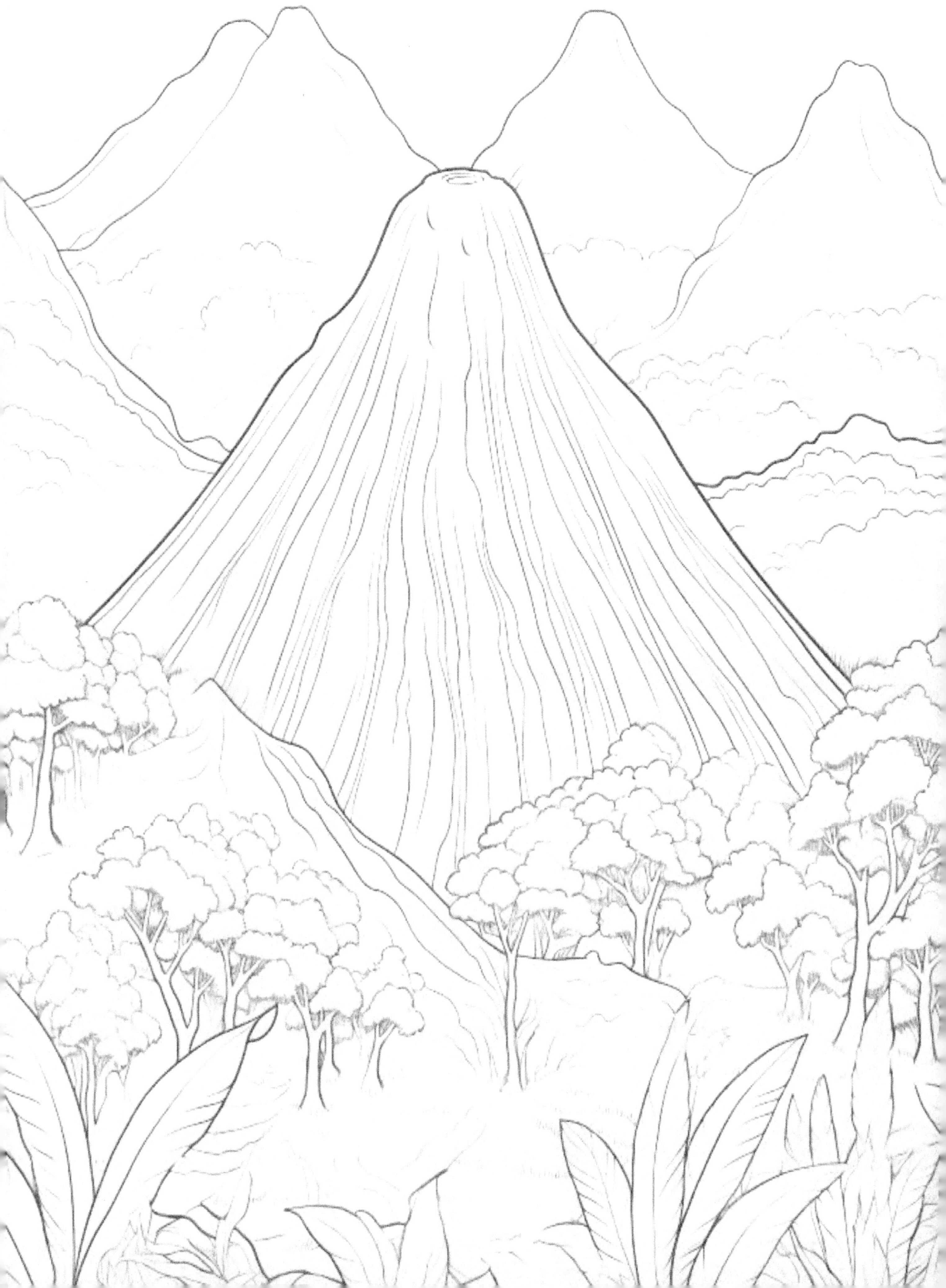

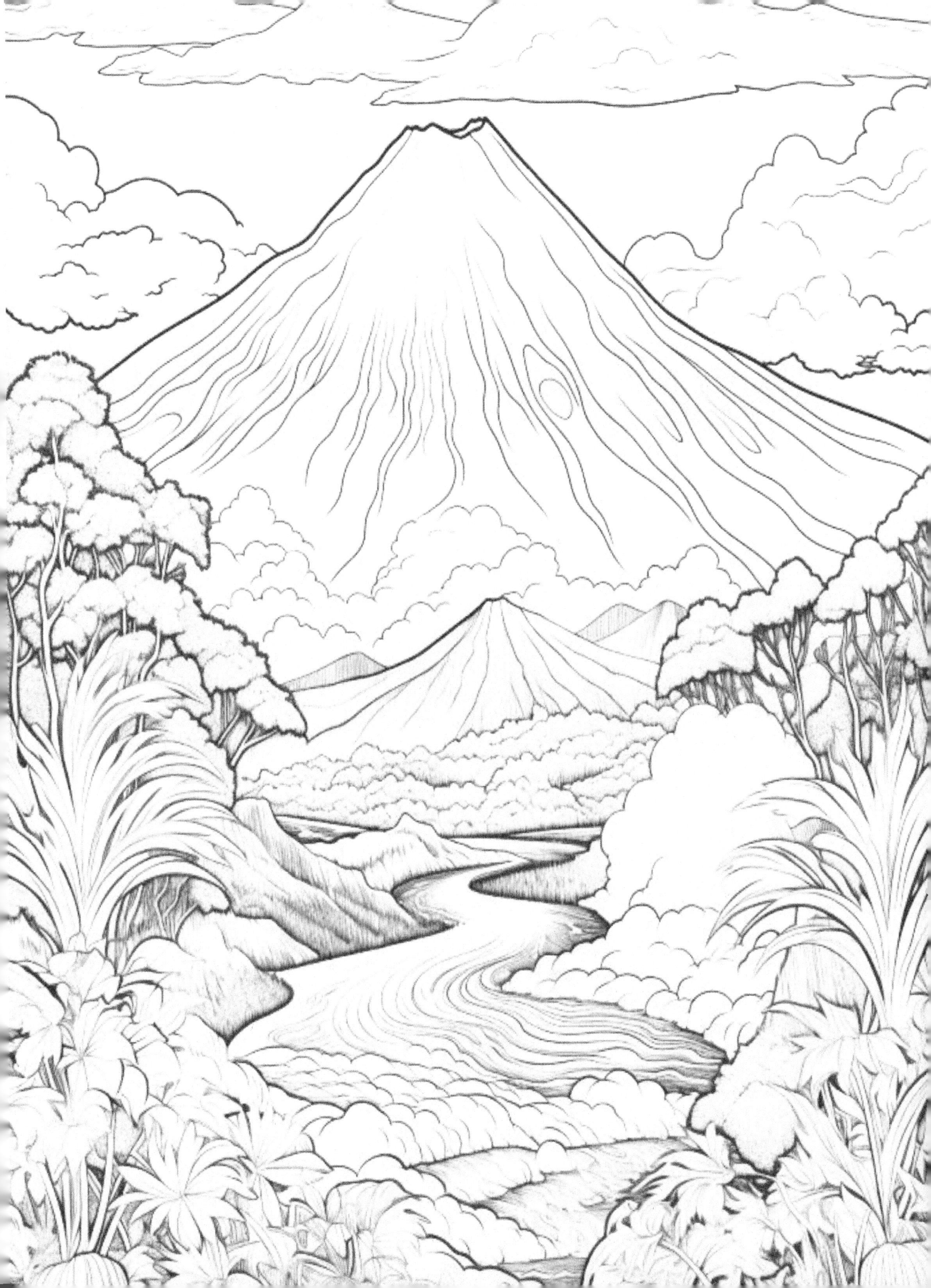

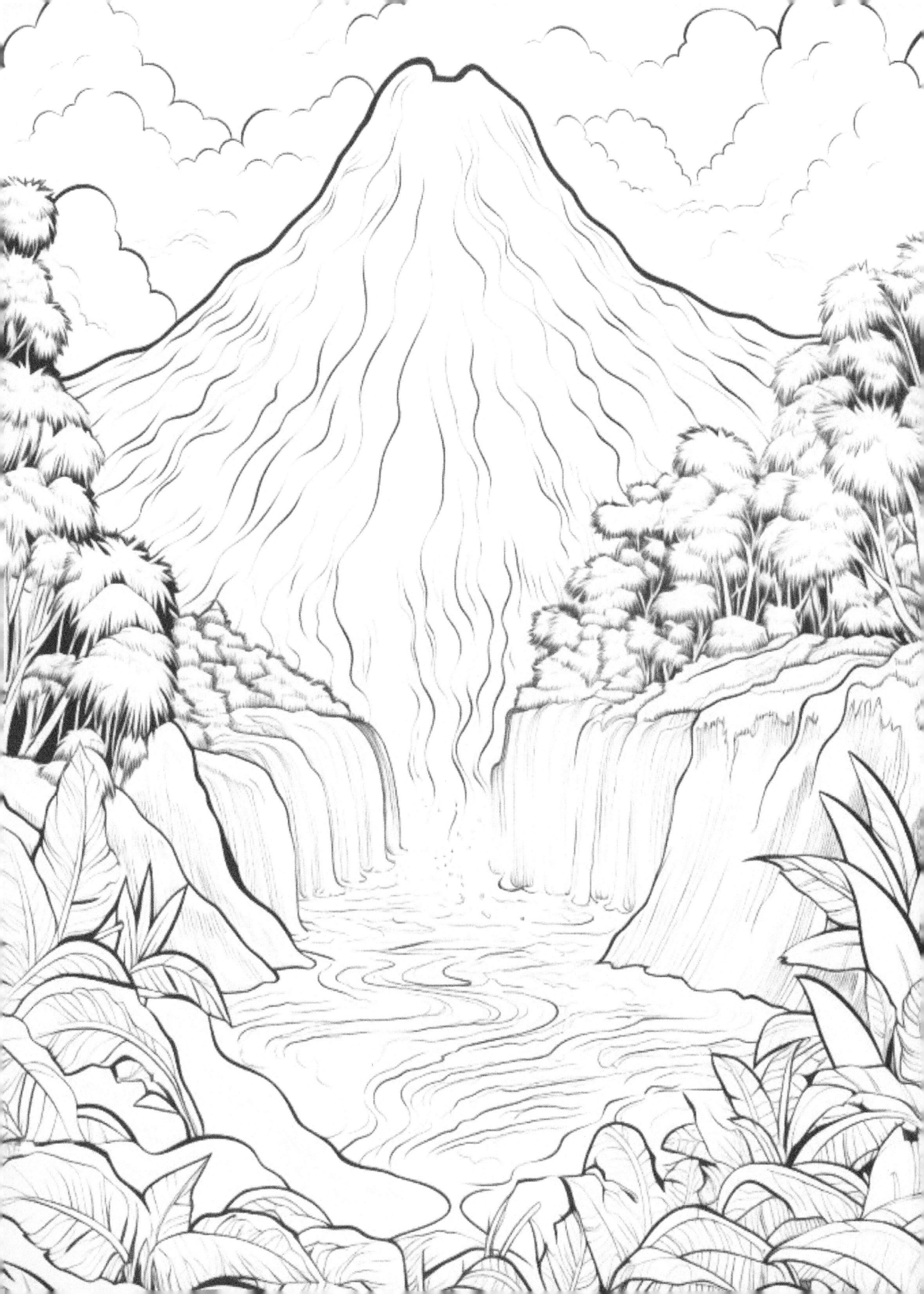

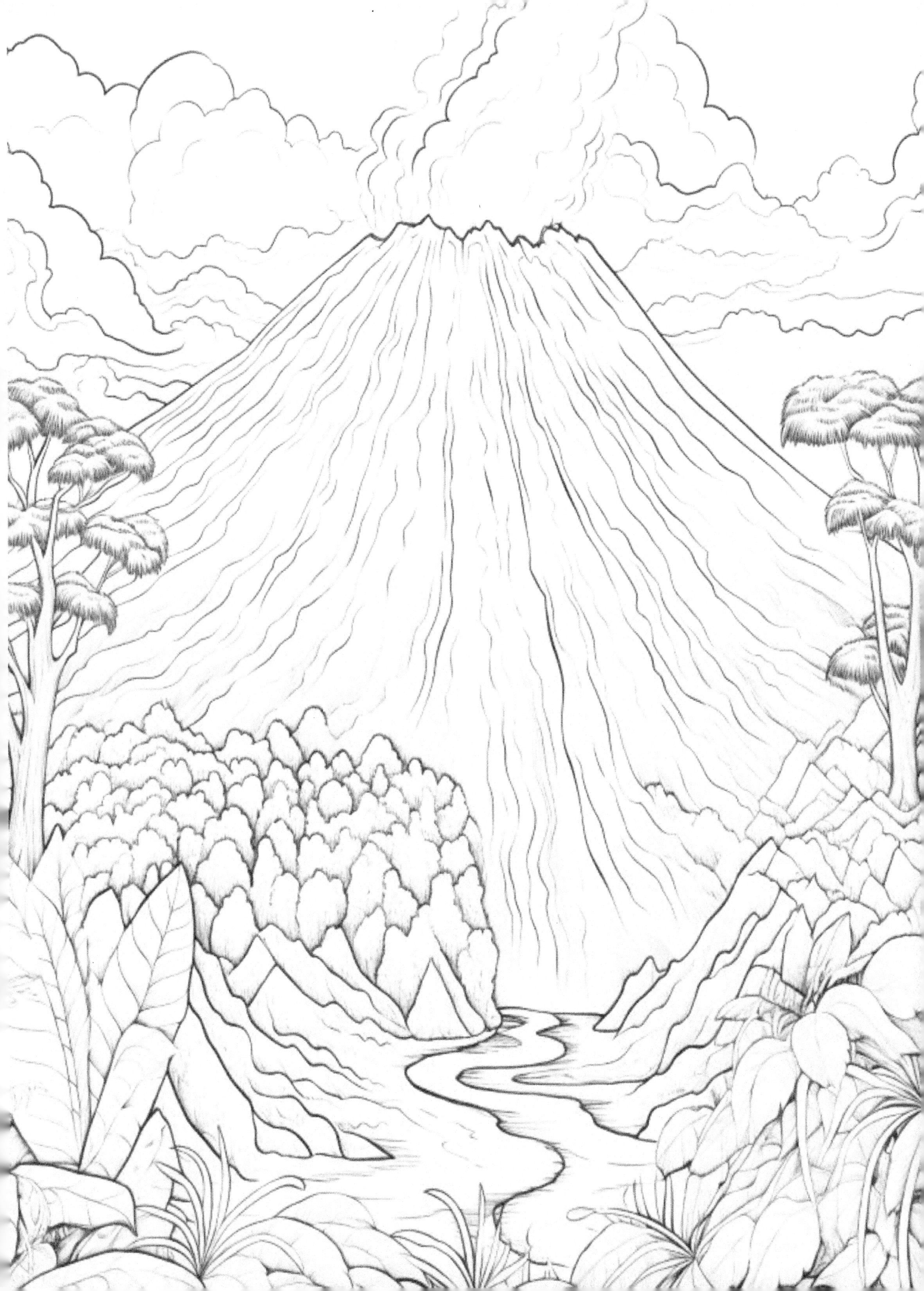

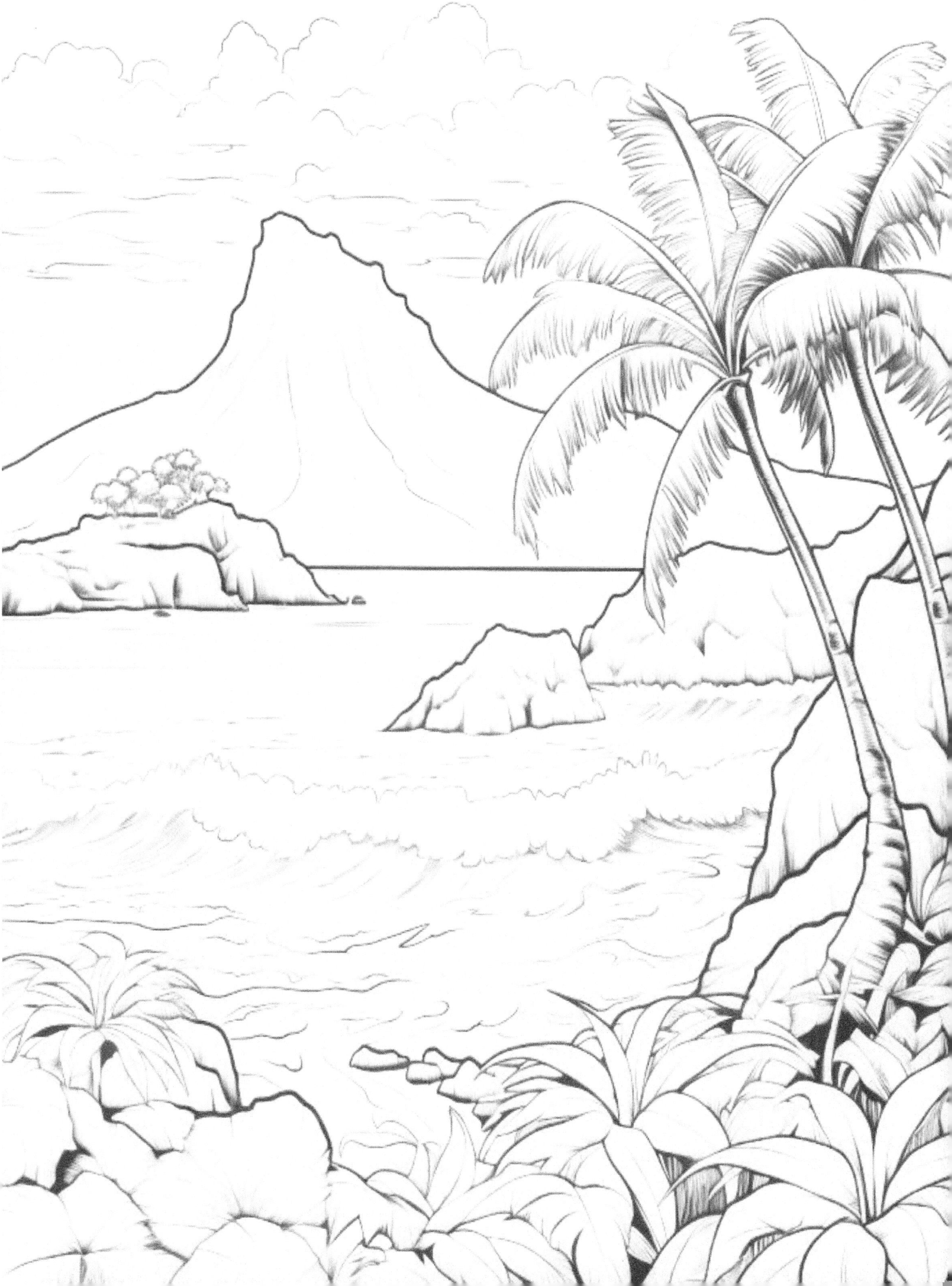

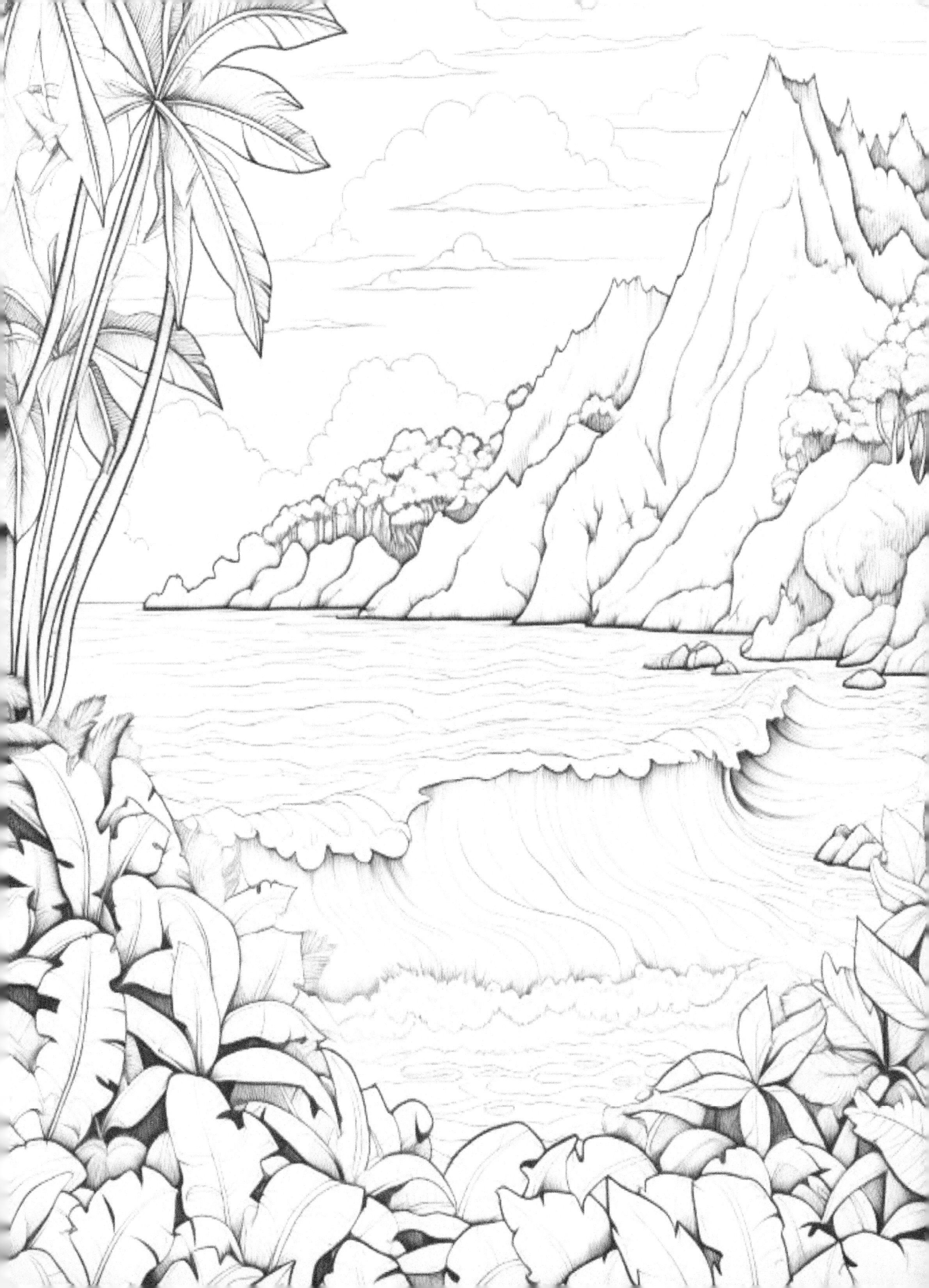

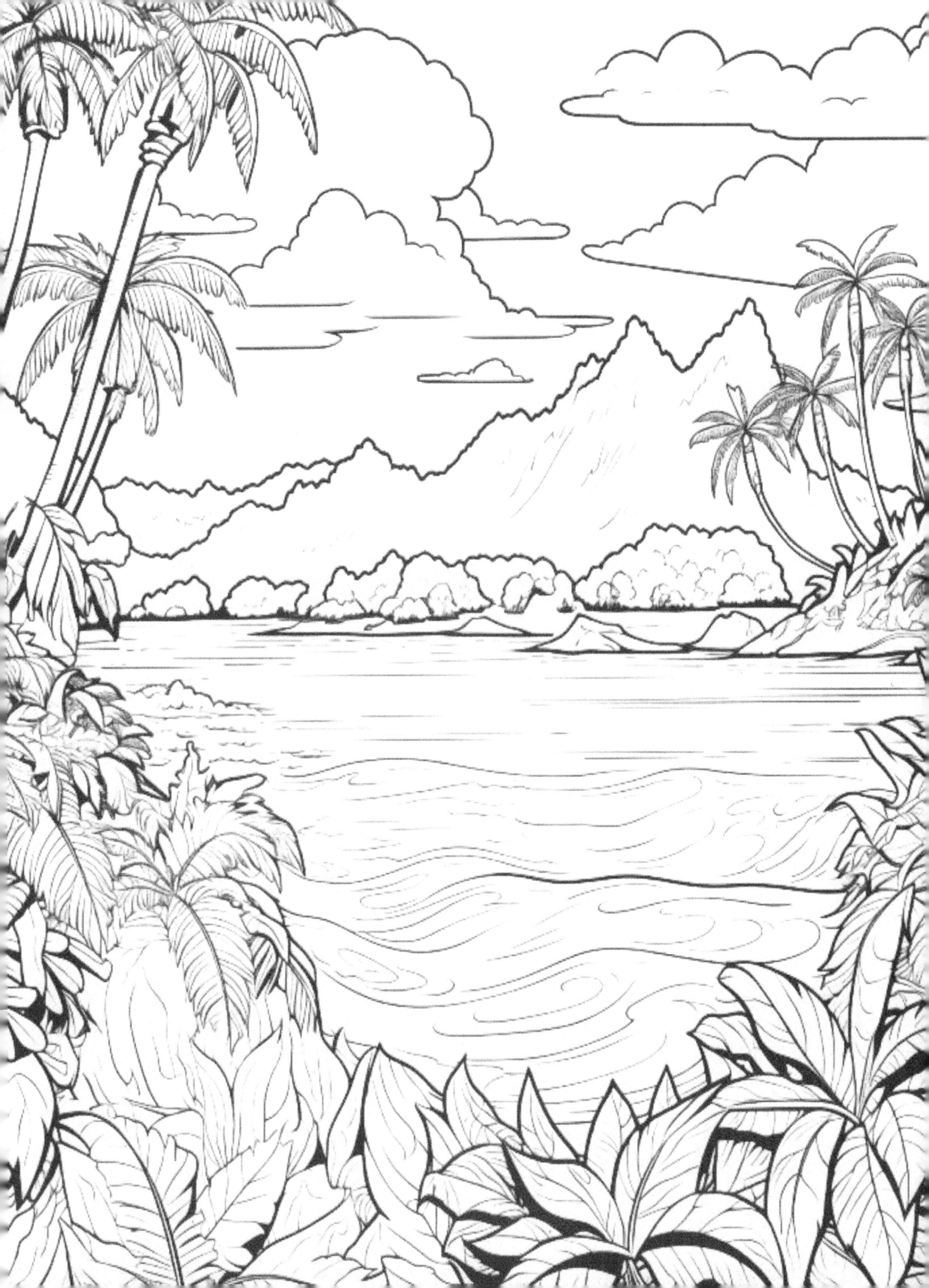

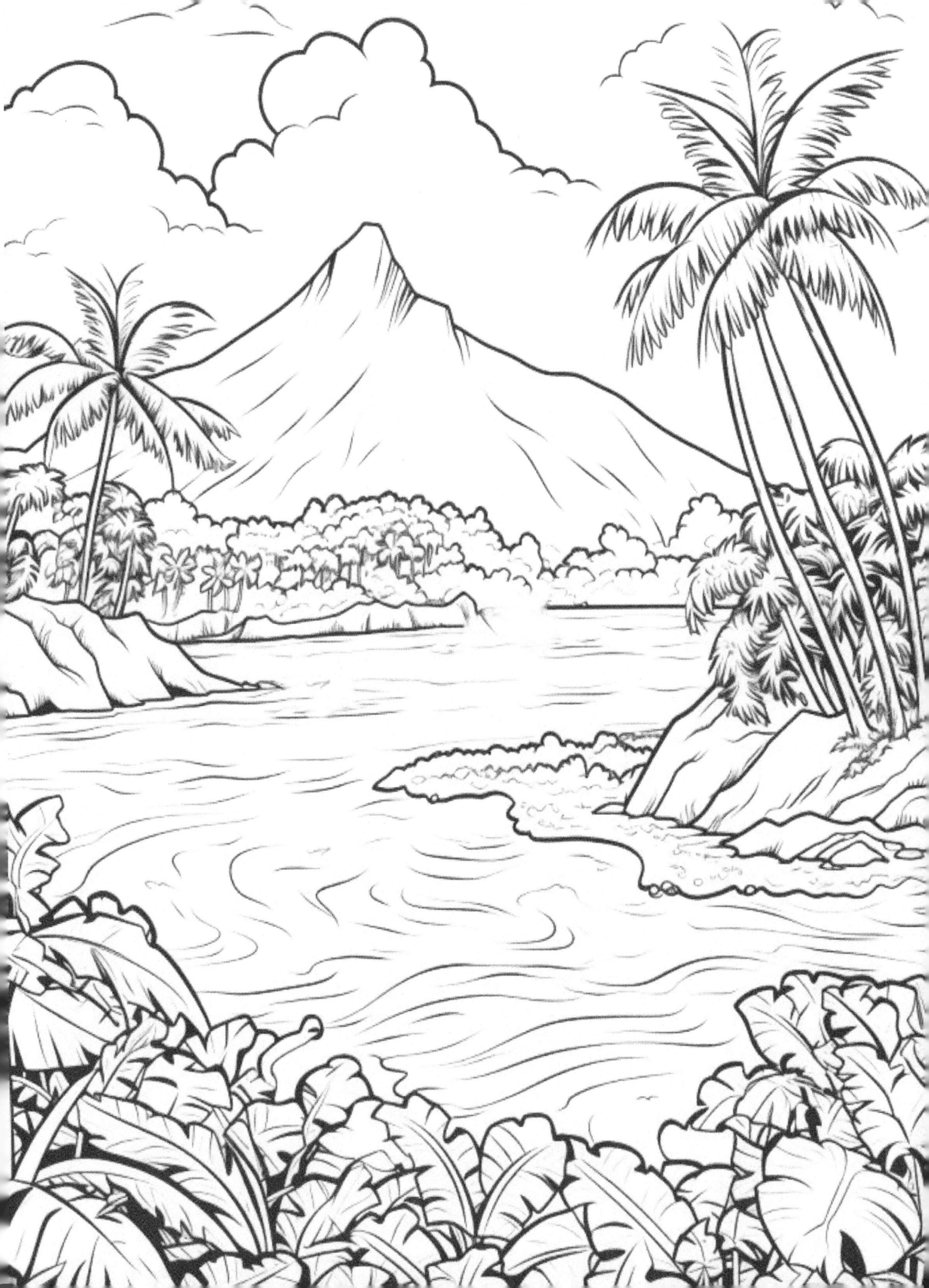

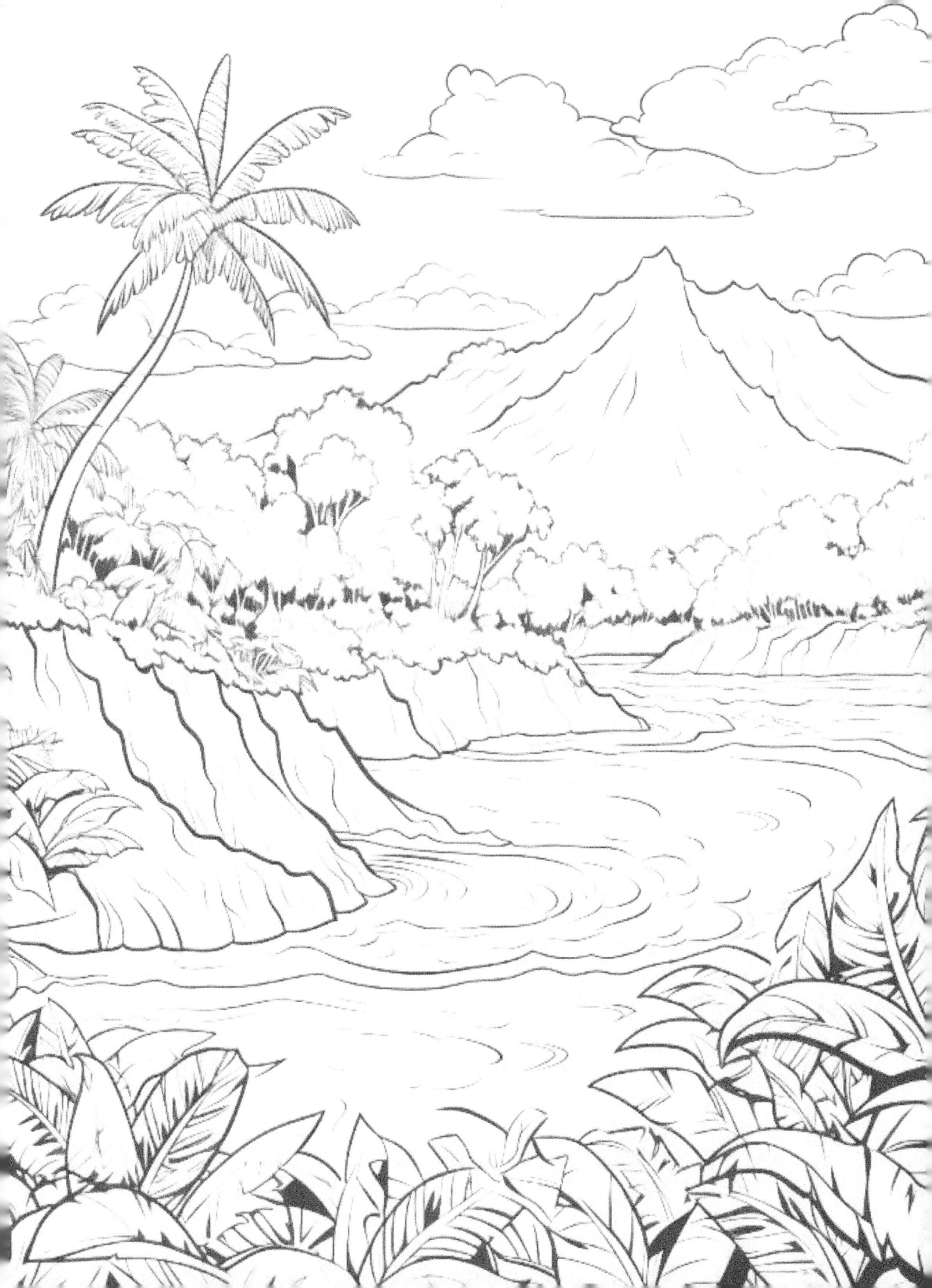

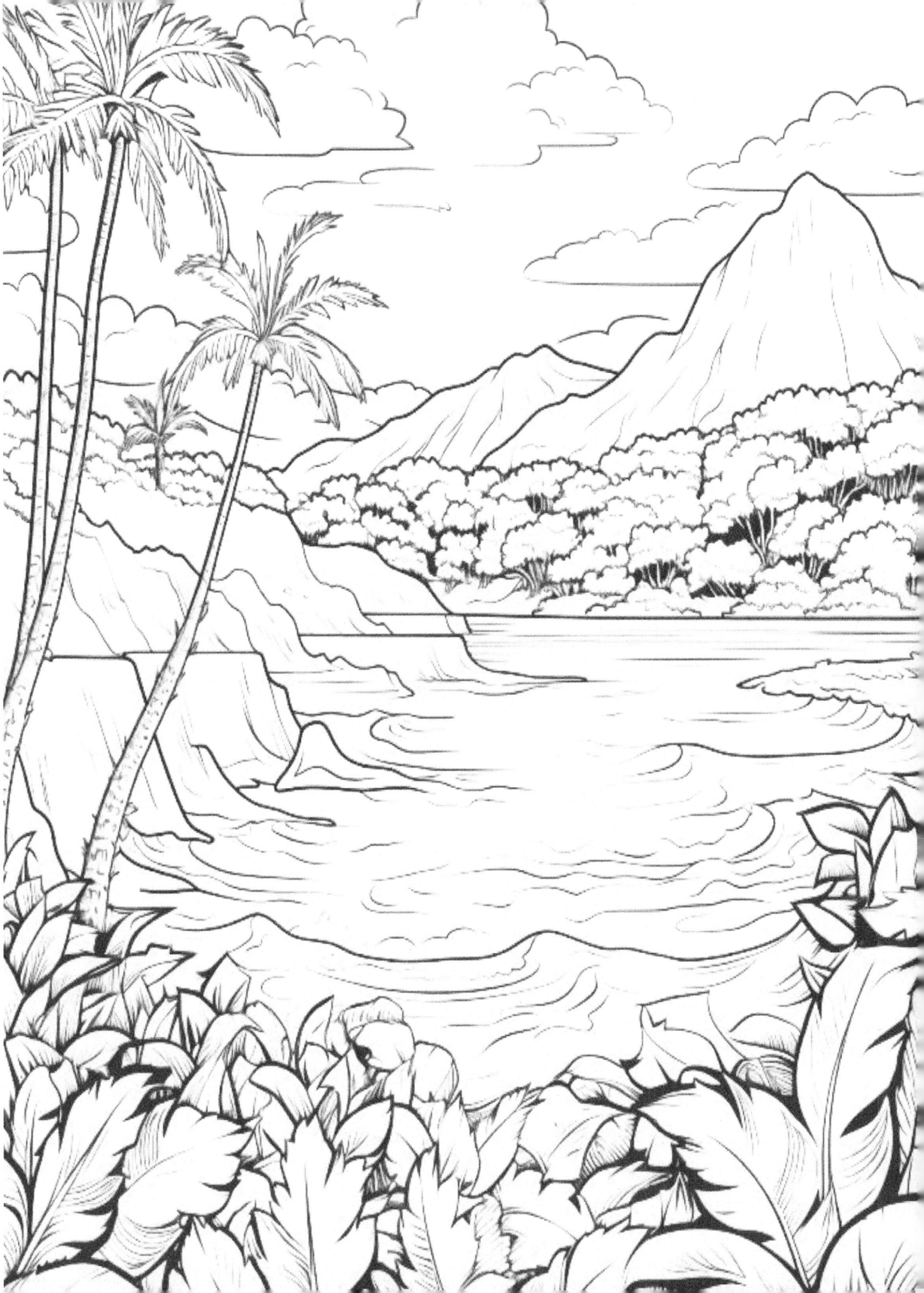

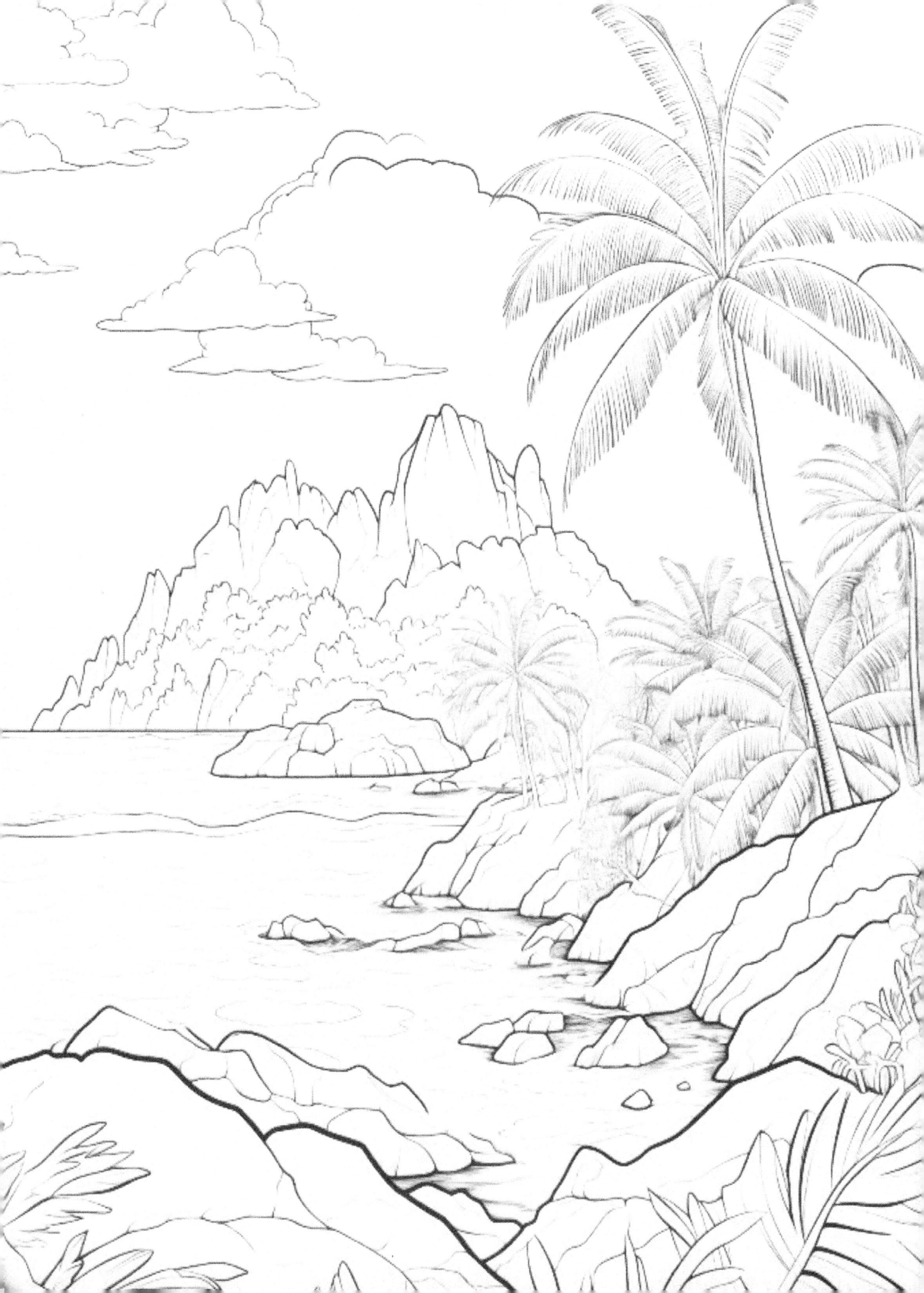

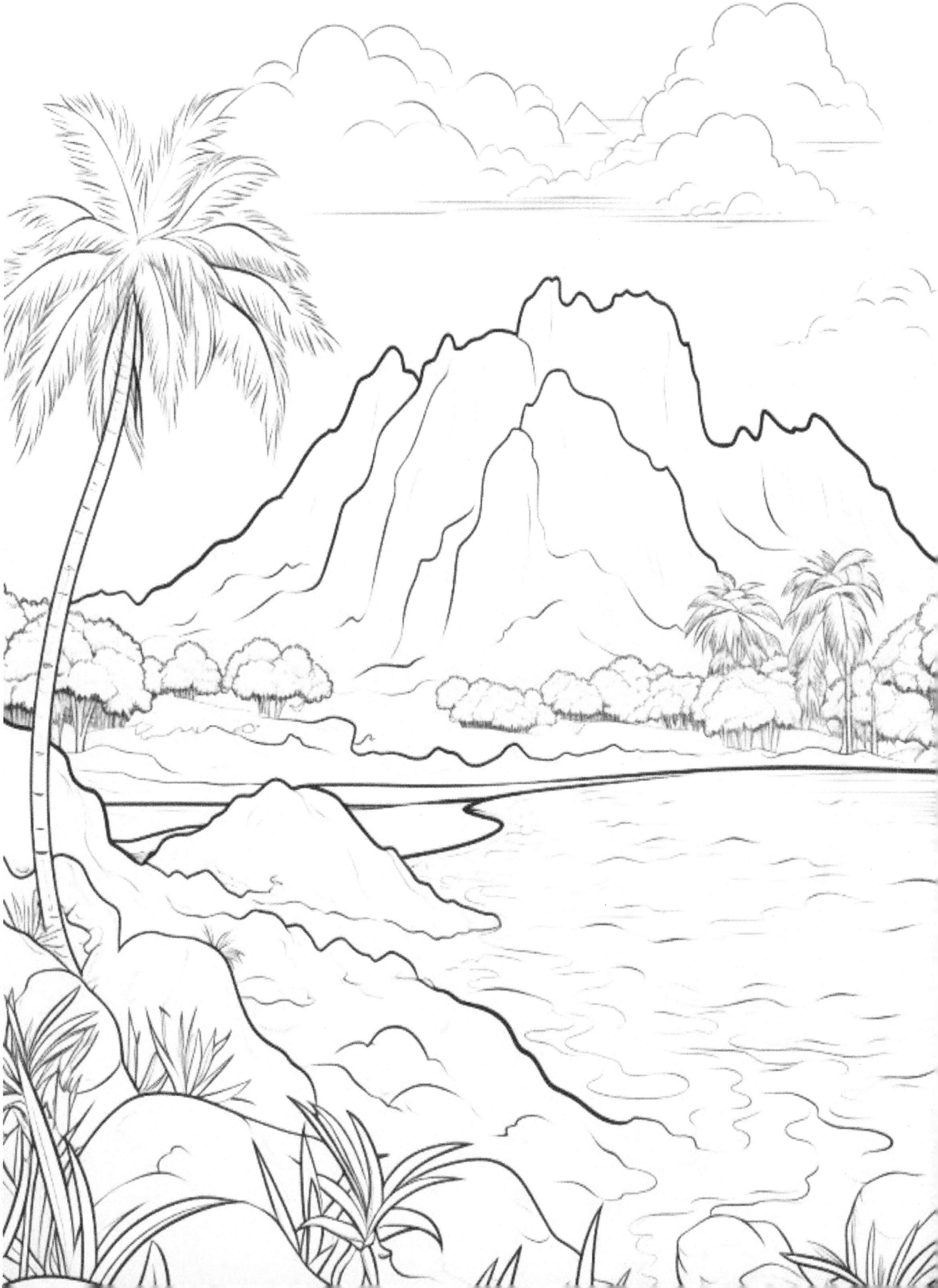

Made in the USA
Coppell, TX
01 December 2024

41486990R00037